LOVE,
LOVE,
LOVE

LOVE, LOVE, LOVE

BY LEN EVANS

LOGOS INTERNATIONAL
Plainfield, NJ

All Scripture references are taken from the King James Version unless otherwise noted as NAS *(New American Standard version).*

To assail the changes that have unmoored us from the past is futile, and, in a deep sense, I think it is wicked. . . . This cannot be an easy life. We shall have a rough time of it to keep our minds open, and to keep them deep . . . in a great, open, windy world; but this is, as I see it, the condition of man; and in this condition we can help, because we can love one another. (J. Robert Oppenheimer)

Table of Contents

LOVE, LOVE, LOVE

Give Me Reality or Give Me Death!

The deepest truth blossoms only from the deepest love. (Heinrich Heine)

"Lord, either give me reality or give me death!" All my pent-up frustrations, anxieties, and broken dreams as a pastor lay behind that cry. It was the year 1960 and my experience in the churches had proven desperately unfulfilling. The aspirations with which I began my ministry in the Presbyterian church had led to complete bewilderment at the promises of God and a lack of fulfillment and excitement that I felt should be found in pastoral ministry.

What was reality? Was it the regular church services I was conducting which were so lacking in excitement and so routinely dull? Worship was not a celebration of joy but a somber exercise, repetitiously boring.

Did we really believe the great gospel of Jesus Christ? Why were not the people greatly excited at the prospect of sharing this good news? Paul had written, "For I am not ashamed of the gospel of Christ: for it is the power of God unto salvation to every one that believeth; to the Jew first, and also to the Greek" (Rom. 1:16). A friend once said: "It may have been power for Paul; it may have been power for Peter; but somewhere the power petered out between Paul, Peter, and myself."

Where had all our dreams gone of an exciting corporate fellowship and ministry? It was easy to see that the people were not profoundly touched by the message of Jesus enough to share that message. In fact, the silence about Jesus and the great, atoning facts of His life would almost indicate a great disproportion between the gospel and their life styles. All the longings of a boy converted to Jesus at the age of eleven, all the hopes of ministering excitingly to a group of turned-on Christians came to a severe halt against the passivity of people who absorbed the message without corresponding excitement and joy. This consistent passivity to the gospel of Jesus completely frustrated me in the pulpit.

Could they believe that Jesus was indeed the Son of God, born of the Virgin Mary, who walked among us as God incarnate, taught superlative truths that need to be lived out, died in a passion of love, and rose in a triumph of God's power and grace? Could they believe these truths and be so indifferent to the expression of them in a world desperately needing to learn and discover the love of God? How could I forget the young married couples of the first pastorate I served reminding me as a

2

graduate seminarian that we were not to become fanatical about the gospel of Jesus! How well I remember an intellectual writer in my first student pastorate telling me that the gospel—from his point of view—was anachronistic to the modern world and was out of date by 100 years.

In a world of endless confrontations between powerful ideologies for which men were willing to give their lives, it seemed to me that we were simply playing church. How discouraging it was to go to board meetings and discuss Boy Scout troops, potluck suppers, the usual details of the church and not see a corresponding commitment to the gospel of Jesus Christ commanding the minds and attention of the people. It was devastating to see the lack of strong enthusiasm for the promulgation of the saving message of Jesus. It was likewise frustrating to see the polarization between ideologies within the church, traditional denominational separation and pride without a corresponding humility of prayer and pleading with God to change the whole situation. Had I studied so many years—including doctoral preparation—to lead a church whose main goals were potluck suppers, ladies' sewing circles, and men involved in the local community with some degree of excitement but seemingly uninterested in the great work of the church?

Analyzing the needs of our modern time to have the gospel of Jesus promulgated with power, we needed a vital lay church in which men aflame with the love of Christ, powerfully attracted to the ministry of the gospel and a sharing witness would literally turn this world

3

upside down with the greatest message the world has ever heard. Why instead did they appear so stoically indifferent and impervious to the absolute joy that the New Testament manifests throughout? How often the statements of J.B. Phillips in the introduction to his single volume on the book of Acts would rankle in my mind. In it he suggested that to turn from the book of Acts to any modern theological writing or traditional or denominational writing would bring tears to one's eyes. He suggested that the early Christians did not have seminars on healing or seminars on prayer, but they moved in vital power to heal and to pray and to touch the hem of God's garment for the needs of their contemporary world. Further, he stated that they might appear unsophisticated to us in their knowledge of the world, but we have to admit they were open to God in a way that is almost totally unknown to our world. This strongly reflected how I felt. Something *was* missing.

Even while at seminary and engaged in doctoral studies where I immersed myself in dialogical questionings and searchings, I sensed they ended in further verbal clarification but did not yield that dynamic which somehow could produce a vibrant and powerful expression of Jesus Christ to our world today. Even the fine attempts of the churches engaged in ecumenical dialogue ended in discussions that did not appear to produce a powerful Christian life style. Where was the promise of much fruit? Why had my own first love for Jesus Christ turned into such gross despair? Where had we all gone so wrong? What would it take to make the church the singing, thrilling witness that our professors had spoken about at seminary?

I had come to the end of my resources. Six or seven years in pastoral ministry seemed bleak with minimal results. Here and there individuals had responded and experienced a conversion to Jesus Christ. The majority, however, seemed content with a routine repetition of worship which led, in my estimation, nowhere.

The world seemed totally indifferent to the church. It patronized the church as a necessary ethical stimulus to its own endeavors, but not sufficiently powerful in itself and in its communication to cause the world to turn and look again at Jesus Christ with new eyes. Our witness seemed almost nonexistent and the preaching of the gospel ineffectual. The indifference of congregations and failure of the people to be aroused to their own message produced deep and pervading futility in the hearts of many clergy. I sensed this wherever I traveled. Even more than indifference to the gospel, I frequently saw a deep-seated hostility between the pew and the pulpit and a low-grade infection of frustration pervading the churches. There was a lack of communication—at times just a toleration—and I frequently observed an actual polarization between groups. The dreams of my heart had been smashed completely and the realities of interpersonal life seemed harshly resistant to the promises of the Word of God. Moreover, I personally encountered two problems I could not surmount. These two problems involved communication and motivation. How do you so communicate the full implications of the gospel of Christ so as to capture the hearts, the wills and the minds of professing Christians and turn them into life-changing witnesses for Christ to the world? After their profession of faith has been made, how does one motivate these same professing Christians to really respond to the total call of God in their lives so that the lay church can touch the world outside with the love and power of the gospel of God? All our efforts seemed blocked by the passivity of the members of the congregation. They assimilated the Word of God without the kind of response that that Word demands. There was something strangely missing. The promise was unfulfilled and unrealized. A strange vacuum existed at the center of church life. It was not altogether bad. Much of it was delightful and good. Much of the fellowship was friendly and satisfying and even loving at times. But it was not alive to the gospel of Christ and the extension of that message in missionary and evangelical persuasiveness in a way that seemed to be demanded by the message itself, and certainly by the needs of the world around it.

My assessment of the church became increasingly dark and pessimistic. I saw nothing that commanded my hope or my life or my being. I had been raised in a strong evangelical background. I had read the deeper life works of many of the outstanding Christians and had sought through this devotional enterprise to enter into some degree of power to communicate the gospel. The disciplines of devotionalism, in my case, had failed to meet the demands of human need. Such exercises had led to culs de sac which had promised much but had yielded little. There was, likewise, a vast polarity in my early days between the so-called liberal and the conservative and fundamentalist. The liberal saw with clarity the gospel implications of compassion in human relationships and the support of human need which can be validated through Scripture. The evangelical saw the absolute necessity for conversion and commitment to Jesus Christ. Both had elements of truth that were biblically sound and I often wondered why there was such a distance between them, why they were not willing to humbly listen to each other and perhaps communicate a whole message which would have been beautiful and powerful.

Intellectually, this frustration produced a deep, "dark night of the soul" for me. The Catholic mystics had spoken of this before and had promised that if one endured the dark night of the soul, one could emerge out of it. That provided some hope of a future experience in God which might bring me out of despair. I had become cold to simplistic theological answers when they did not meet the high demands of human living. The prospect of twenty-five or thirty more years in the ministry was bleak indeed. Hope that this could be changed seemed impossible against the years of struggle.

Some did respond to the gospel. We formed ourselves into small Bible classes. We studied the Word with eagerness and joy. We became knowledgeable about many teachings of the Word of God; we shared with delight our increased insights, but still something was missing in the inner dimensions of our lives and interpersonal relationships. Moreover, these small groups represented only a cellular part of the total church body.

In time, hope postponed can lead to deep despair. Hope promised, but not realized, can lead to massive frustration. Eventually, I was immersed in both of these.

There seemed to be no way out. I had observed church life broadly and the political maneuvering of many within the churches. I had witnessed the absence of a quality of caring among many who professed the name of Jesus. All this added up to an inner futility which seemed insurmountable to me. The polarities within the Christian communities seemed irresolvable and irreconcilable. I was literally at my wit's end and at the end of all my resources. Reading theology, history, and devotional literature became dissatisfying, because the human condition seemed unchangeable.

On a marvelous day when I was alone in my study at the Roseville Presbyterian Church in Newark, New Jersey, looking deep within to an emptiness I could not counter, looking without to an environment that seemed so bleak, I realized I could not go on as I was. I threw myself on the floor of my study and cried in utter despair to the Savior I loved—who at times seemed so distant from my need—"Lord, either give me reality or give me death!"

What was reality? I believed in Jesus Christ as my Savior with all my heart. I believed in the great message of the gospel with all my might. Yet the promise of power for communication of the gospel and of that quality of life which He promises was lacking. There was some key that I could not find to explain the vacuum both in my own heart and at the center of corporate church experience. The exercise of my mind had led me to intellectual bankruptcy. The great theological systems I studied seemed to lead to the same dead end. My cry was desperation itself. It is a beautiful truth of the Word of God "that whosoever shall call on the name of the Lord shall be saved" (Acts 2:21). This does not only mean salvation as we understand it but that God so summoned will come to our aid when we realize our need for Him. Without Him nothing can ever be successful.

Little did I know this cry would become a watershed experience for me. Little did I realize the tremendous adventure that would follow that cry, the agonistic searchings that still lay ahead and the fulfillments that would lie so far beyond my wildest dreams. Little did I understand that day that I was crying out for the Holy Spirit to come to my rescue. Little did I perceive the answer lay so close at hand and yet so far removed and distant. How good God is. It is still true that His strength is perfected in weakness, His power operates through broken vessels, His wisdom superlatively transcends the finest thinking of man. Jesus provides all the answers but I did not yet know how He would provide them for me.

2

Discovery

And to know the love of Christ, which passeth knowledge, that ye might be filled with all the fulness of God. (Eph. 3:19)

"Your father looks like Arthur Treacher to me." My wife always said this about dad who was certainly the dominant figure in our home. Born Harold H. Evans on June 25, 1876, in Birmingham, England, he was to know the cultured, scholarly life of the affluent and wealthy. Their home was a palatial one with maids, cooks, gardeners, and chauffeurs. Eventually he came to the United States and found lodging in a boarding house operated by my aunt and uncle in Chicago. Here he met and later married my mother, Florence Elizabeth Morrey, who was born also in Chicago and grew up in a fine Methodist background. One year later I was born on November 28, 1921, and my brother Robert Charles, eighteen months afterwards.

Our home was a good home, filled with the warmth of

mother's love and the deep integrity and intellection of my father. It was basically a happy, creative place. The kitchen was certainly the center of our living. Here we dined, played games, enjoyed good discussions together. As a very little boy I can remember being challenged to memorize details of geography and to perform mathematical equations in my head. Each week we were taken to the local library to select good reading. Eventually I was given piano lessons. Very early, mother, herself a secretary, taught me how to type.

Father was Anglican by background and tradition but not church oriented. Although he did not attend church at all that I could remember, my brother and I were sent to a local Presbyterian church. Frequently in the evenings, however, I recall my father would sit at a circular table in the dining room and read the Bible in both the original Greek and Hebrew. He had studied Greek at Oxford University and had taught himself Hebrew. For hours each night he pored over the Scriptures. Employed at a local drugstore on the south side of Chicago, each week his employer who apparently was a fine Christian gentleman, Mr. Williams, would come to our home for Bible study and conversation with my parents.

The first eight years of my life were tranquil enough. Worldwide depression—which struck in 1929—would alter that immeasurably. We were introduced to poverty, welfare, and the Works Projects Administration. In spite of this, our home was still one of dignity and support.

Poverty is a crushing load to be borne in the hearts of

men. We saw it affect our parents deeply and it bred in my heart a sense of inferiority and need. Poverty was a common experience in those days. My heart will ever be grateful to God for exactly these experiences for they taught us to care for those in need and were to lead eventually to a search for a gospel large enough to meet the broad needs of our fellow-man.

Small events are in the hand of God and His purposes are secreted behind the natural turning points of our lives. One day while a student at the O'Toole Grammar School on the south side of Chicago, a young classmate by the name of Walter Puhr invited my brother and me to the Laflin Street Gospel Hall. He explained that if he could bring the largest number of children to Rally Day Sunday school he would receive a very expensive fountain pen and pencil set as a reward. So it was on a Sunday afternoon we first attended this small Plymouth Brethren assembly. These lovely Scottish people warmly received all the children and consequently we made it our church home. They, of course, were eager to present the claims of Christ to all of the children.

For this purpose they had invited Alfred P. Gibbs, a missionary of many years' experience, and a Pied Piper with children, to give a series of children's gospel meetings. This he did, using Bunyan's *Pilgrim's Progress* as a vehicle. Accompanied by slides of great beauty, he told the story of the pilgrim's search for eternal life and the truth of salvation. Each successive Friday night hundreds of children poured into that chapel to hear the recounting of the story of Christ clothed in this picturesque way. The missionary himself

13

was an attractive person. We wiggled and we squirmed but we heard the message.

Pilgrim's Progress is the story of a man who becomes aware of the passing of time and the transience of life, who bears on his back a tremendous load which he must carry and from which no one has the power to release him. Symbolically, it represents accumulated guilt and sin. Weighed down by this load, he seeks unsuccessfully for relief. Eventually he learns about a person called Jesus who has the power to relieve people of their burdens. He meets a preacher who was an officer in Cromwell's army in England. The cleric begins to point him to eternal life. Puzzled by his lack of awareness of this message and seeking to discover it, he does not know how to begin searching. Encouraged by the pastor who is called Evangelist, he begins his search for God. While proceeding through many phases of search and adventure, he goes through a tremendous Slough of Despond. As children, we were thrilled to watch this allegory developed so intriguingly by this man who loved children.

Aided out of the Slough of Despond by a man called Helps, Pilgrim was later to detour to the village of Morality and nearly lose his way. Warned again by Evangelist to seek no other answer than that of God he is redirected on his way to a Wicket Gate. Passing through this gate, he travels, still searching, until he comes to a hill called Calvary.

Hardly did I realize that night, as a little eleven-year-old boy, that God himself would lay His hand upon me. As the missionary spoke the words of

Romans 1:16, and told the story of Jesus Christ and His great life and marvelous, atoning love, I was to drift out of the message and to weep my way into the arms of God. No longer was I listening to the words of a man. Suddenly faith was born in my heart.

I cannot explain how faith comes; it is truly a gift of God. The facts that were being presented in the story became true in my heart. God loved me that much! God sent His only Son into the world to die for the sins of the world—including my own. God had mightily raised His Son in a triumph and victory beyond any human imagining. The missionary was saying that our sins could be forgiven, that we could become the children of God by faith if we would only accept the offer of eternal life through Christ. We could invite this Jesus into our hearts and experience sonship in the family of God. I could hardly see the pictures through the tears that lay like pools in my eyes, reflecting the deep emotional turbulence of my heart.

When the meeting was over I ran to the front to speak to Mr. Gibbs. Was it true that Jesus loved me so much? The missionary reassured me that He did, and he appointed a Scottish gentleman to take me to a little room in the front of the hall to explain again the good news, the wonder of eternal life granted to anyone who would believe, and the simplicity of faith. We knelt together and at the suggestion of this older man, I repeated a simple prayer confessing my sins and thanking Jesus for having died on my behalf. Whereupon, at the end of the prayer—on my own—I went on to thank God for raising Jesus from the dead. At this point an unbelievable joy broke upon my heart and my tears mingled with a joy that I've never forgotten though it happened many years ago. That night will always remain indelibly impressed upon my memory. I knew without controversy that I had met the risen Christ in the depths of my being. I literally ran from that room to my home experiencing such joy that my feet scarcely touched the pavement. Dashing into the kitchen where mother and dad were playing chess, I announced without preparation that I had been born again and saved.

Now when you tell your educated, Anglican father that you have been born again, he is subject to trauma. I will never know what my father actually thought that night but he wisely sent his son to bed.

During subsequent weeks and months, my very shrewd and perceptive father watched me with extreme interest. Eventually, being convinced that his son had stumbled upon a secret that he himself had not learned or discovered—a well of joy that he could not reproduce—he attended the little church. There the good news of salvation became clear to him and he gradually turned over his whole life to Jesus as his Savior and Lord. Father's experience produced tremendous changes in our home and life style. His was no momentary conversion. He knew of no specific date when he had committed his life to Christ. Nevertheless, even though it was progressive there is no doubt that it was a radical conversion experience. Christ commanded the whole being of this tremendous man. All of his studies in the Hebrew and Greek Bible suddenly were focused on the newly acquired key to understanding. His whole heart was caught up in Christ as a strong man's heart should be.

My father became, in my personal estimation as a layman, the finest witness for Christ I have ever known. In spite of his English austerity, he combined an ardent love for the Bible and a great desire to win people for Jesus Christ. He not only led a great number to Christ through his personal integrity and witness, but he would spend years training them in the Word of God itself.

I saw, through my father's witness, the power of Jesus Christ to transform personalities, to radically change the direction of men's lives. What a magnetic power Christ exerts in the hearts of strong men and women to shape them into something beautiful. So there was born in my heart the desire to be a pastor and to preach the good news and to bring men to Christ.

Two men fostered this desire in me. James Humphrey, a lay preacher, would take me as a boy to share my testimony wherever he preached. J. Bruce Slack, a Baptist pastor, would spend hours with me in the Bible and prayer. They invested in a young man's life. My father would take me as a teen-ager, along with the Christian Business Men's Committee, to witness in missions, jails, and on street corners.

I was timid by nature and to stand in my own neighborhood to declare my faith on a street corner intimidated me. Having been exposed to the power of the gospel in so many ways, my quiet desire to preach was intensified. How very grateful I am to my evangelical friends for taking the time to nurture me in the faith, thereby developing within me a passionate and continuing hunger for evangelism.

Unfortunately, along with this beautiful emphasis on the saving power of Jesus Christ, they unconsciously communicated a negative message to me. The very strength of their evangelicalism sometimes limited their perspectives. A spirit of intolerance was imperceptibly developed and it was subtly communicated concerning others who did not take a similar position. For example, fear of Roman Catholics and Catholic theology was imparted, a strong anti-liberalism was maintained, and a fear of denominationalism developed. They were truly afraid of the historical denominations.

Another aspect of this whole teaching was to produce a ghetto mentality whereby we were withdrawn from the great secular and, at times, religious concerns of the broader life stream. Thinking to maintain a purer clarity of vision, we sometimes imbibed a spiritual orthodoxy which tended to withdraw from others and the world itself. Being gospel-centered, we primarily saw people as "objects" for salvation.

Likewise, I remember no sermons on the Holy Spirit during all the years in which I grew up. Christology was emphasized and the doctrine of salvation was repetitively asserted, but pneumatology, or the doctrine of the Holy Spirit, was largely ignored. Little emphasis was placed on family living.

Nonetheless, these were happy, growing years. The Bible was the center of study. Although it was sometimes dispensationalized too much, a beauty of the Word of God crept into our hearts.

My high school years were extremely happy. Because of my musical training I was in the center of the exciting groups of leadership. With college as a goal, my studies consisted of the liberal arts and academic courses.

The Depression was just turning around in 1939 when I graduated from high school. Too poor to attend college, even though a scholarship was available, I looked for a job. There was none to be found for a long time. I tried to make money by playing the organ in funeral chapels and for weddings but this was insufficient for my needs. Eventually, I secured employment with the Rexall Drug Company which maintained a large office and distribution center in Chicago. Shortly after this my father and my brother were hired, and the economic situation in our home was greatly changed.

One Sunday afternoon my good friend, Pastor Bruce Slack, and I had just returned from witnessing in a suburb west of Chicago. The radio was turned on and suddenly, without preparation, the announcer declared that we were at war with Japan. It was December 7, 1941. We were being acquainted for the first time with the sober facts of the Japanese air attack on Pearl Harbor. How well I remember standing alone in the front room of our apartment knowing immediately that the course of our personal destiny would be greatly affected by World War II.

In 1942 I enlisted, with two friends, in the United States Navy and we were stationed at the Glenview Naval Air Station just outside of Chicago. Here, as later in the navy, we were to encounter many fine, young

Christian men and women in the Navigators and other Christian associations.

3

Preparation

Love is ever the beginning of knowledge, as fire is of light. (Thomas Carlyle)

Being uprooted from a very controlled home life and thrust into a naval career during a major world war was both threatening and exciting. The Glenview Naval Air Station, with its "country club" setting, was a beautiful place to begin training. Curiously, I met a large number of Christian sailors both in the personnel office in which I worked and in the Naval Air Station choir with which I sang. Musicians of outstanding ability and concert stature performed with this choir. It was while we were singing in one of the churches in Chicago that I met Elizabeth Marie Anderson who was to become my wife. A courtship of several months followed. It was my fear that if I didn't claim her before I was shipped out that some other sailor might come along, see what I had seen, and snatch her away from me.

One Sunday morning while I was playing the organ for the church services at the air station, the Chief of Naval Chaplains observed me. He later wrote a letter from the Pentagon requesting that I transfer my rating from yeoman, second class, to specialist W, second class, which was chaplain's assistant. This I was willing to do, but I asked if I might have enough time to secure an engagement ring for Bette before I left. The Pentagon granted me that time!

After chaplain's assistant training school, I was assigned to a very large training center in Farragut, Idaho. This base was situated in the beautiful Rocky Mountains near two clear inland lakes, Pend Oreille and Coeur d'Alene. Again I experienced the refreshing of Christian fellowship in a group of single and married couples associated with the Navigators. What marvelous evenings we spent in each other's company, sharing our Christian faith. I still vividly recall crisp winter nights in the married couples' barracks where we usually met. God was gradually broadening my awareness and stretching my mind to see His marvelous ecumenical love.

While Christian fellowship was supportive, my thoughts and emotions continued to turn back to Chicago and to Bette. At the advice of some older friends who recognized the romantic longings of a young sailor, I called Bette and asked her if she would marry me. Terribly timid and afraid she might say no, I vividly remember that long distance call. To my amazement, she accepted my proposal and on March 29, 1944, we were married at the Midwest Bible Church in Chicago by Torrey M. Johnson.

Our tour of duty as newlyweds in Farragut, Idaho, was extremely pleasant. At its completion, we were transferred to the Radar Training School in Fort Lauderdale, Florida. Toward the end of the war I was assigned to the Naval Hospital Rehabilitation Center in Palm Beach, Florida, and then mustered out in December of 1945, rejoining my wife who had already returned to Chicago.

Although Bette had hoped to marry a businessman rather than a pastor, we had agreed that God was calling me to the ministry. Shortly before the winter semester I applied at Wheaton College and at Northwestern University. Wheaton responded that they could not accept me until the next semester, but Northwestern University sent a telegram that I could begin immediately in January of 1946. Knowing that I would go on to Princeton Theological Seminary, we chose courses at Northwestern which we felt would be a good preparation toward that end. Our major course of study included Greek, Latin, and classical languages and we minored in philosophy. In the discipline of philosophy (our keenest interest) we explored the writings of the great idealists and the modern moods stemming from existentialism. For many years we would struggle with the powerful mind and analysis of Immanuel Kant in his *Critique of Pure Reason.* We also sensed the power of the scientific approach to obtain facts of immense meaning. It was not long, however, before we also recognized the great intellectual antagonism to the evangelical emphases of our early upbringing. We were literally overwhelmed by the brilliance of the minds we encountered at the university and thrilled by the great literature of the ages.

It was the thinking of the German philosopher, Immanuel Kant, that became a battleground in my own mind. In his developed concepts he seemed to say that all we could know was what we could think, and that our life experience was somehow restricted to the intellectual and the conceptual. A feeling of powerlessness began to attack my mind. If all we can know is what we can think it seemed to me that we were dreadfully limited. These ideas raised many questions. Are there not other avenues to knowledge? I wondered. I wanted to discover if revelation as it is described in the Word of God is an avenue to knowing what is beyond the scientific method of discovery. My battle with the mind of Kant lasted for ten years.

It was while I was at the university that I began to sense the failure of the idealists to come up with a comprehensive system for the meaning and purpose of life. Through the powerful mind of Soren Kierkegaard, the father of modern existentialism, I sensed the limited approach of the idealists and the modern mood that was to develop. I knew as well, however, that the existentialist "plunge into being" could no more elicit final truth than the idealist's tendency to systematize life. I believed that Jesus Christ was the answer to life—God's answer to life—but I still questioned how this was so. It seemed to me that the church was not living up to its potentialities. I could not see the modern church making the kind of impact upon the world that I felt was mandatory if Jesus Christ was to be seen by the modern intellect as the key to the answers for which the world seeks.

The university years were beautiful for Bette and me. We always enjoyed each other's company and the intellectual stimulus of study was important to both of us. Many searching questions were forming in our minds. These had to do with the relationship of the Christian to his world and the role and function of the Christian in his position in the world. More questions were engendered than were, in fact, answered. Kant's powerful analysis of epistemology raised many interesting questions. Hopefully, seminary would provide some of the answers for which we sought.

Armed with my Phi Beta Kappa key, after graduating cum laude, and with high anticipations, we set out early one morning and drove in leisurely fashion to Princeton, New Jersey, a beautiful college community. The great Princeton University, the Advanced Center for Research, the RCA Research Laboratories, the tremendous intellectual climate, and our goal—Princeton Theological Seminary, the "mecca" for those in training for the Presbyterian ministry—made this charming town an exciting place to live and study. How delighted we were to be at this point in the progress toward our goal.

I soon found myself attached to a very fine professor, Dr. Emile Cailliet, Stuart Professor of Christian Philosophy. We were to become almost like father and son as well as professor and student. I later became his teaching fellow in Christian philosophy.

Being already oriented to academic discipline, I studied hard and enjoyed exploring the minds of leading European and American theologians. My own professor expanded my mind to see the majesty of a great, creative God who was Lord, not only of salvation, but of the universe and of all knowledge. He expanded my scope and my vision. Being of a somewhat mystical temperament, he combined mysticism in a marvelous way with the power of a brilliant mind. Together we studied the writings of Blaise Pascal, the Roman Catholic Jansenist, who was also an early existentialist. We drew in the evidence of science along with the study of theology. We explored the implications of quantum physics through the work of Max Planck and we learned about Heisenberg's principle of indeterminacy. We studied the relationship of the great literature of the ages to theological thought. We explored together the great historical, theological traditions and developments. Always there was the excitement of learning something more applicable and relevant to our own condition.

At the same time, however, I was experiencing a gradual intellectual disturbance. In our attempt to make the gospel relevant to the present day, it seemed to me that we were making it increasingly irrelevant. Dr. Charles Malik, former president of the Economic Council of the United Nations, had commented to the churchmen that we in the church had made the great mistake of permitting the secular world to postulate both the questions and the answers for our age. I began to suspect that the church's constant search for relevancy was making the gospel have decreasing impact.

As we studied the great theological systems of thought—for example, the demythologizing approach of Rudolph Bultmann—I had the strangest feeling that we were actually distancing ourselves from powerful, productive Christianity. We were belaboring the intellectual systematization of Christianity but losing its powerful dynamic. We were ethicizing the great supernatural facts of the Bible, but losing the simple message of the gospel. A gradual sense of restlessness came over me. As I heard contrasting points of view presented by different professors on campus I sensed again the insecurities of contemporary theology. Later, the president of the seminary wrote to graduates that, in effect, modern theology was in a shambles, that the great systems of theological thought we had pursued had not produced great Christianity, great churchmanship, great discipleship, or great preaching. This sense of restless dissatisfaction accompanied my studies while in seminary.

It was for this reason I decided to enter graduate school beyond seminary and pursue the course of theological studies still further. Always there was the hope that perhaps I would discover a further key and new insights that would make the gospel more relevant to our times.

Dr. Cailliet accepted me as a graduate student and teaching fellow. For the next two years I assisted him in the department and completed my studies toward the comprehensive examinations for a doctorate in theology. I took these and passed. Dr. Cailliet assigned

27

me this dissertation topic: "A Comparative Study of Hegel's Concept of Dialectic and Kierkegaard's Concept of Repetition." Somehow this assignment did not excite me!

During those two years while I was a teaching fellow in Christian philosophy at Princeton I was also a student pastor in a small Presbyterian church in New York. We would drive for several hours from Princeton to my weekend charge. This was my first exposure to church life from the level of pastoral responsibility. How well I remember when one of the leaders of that intellectual community accosted me with the accusation that I was preaching a message geared to the nineteenth century and was not up-to-date. In anger, I shot back, "I do not think you understand nineteenth-century theology!"

What had really troubled me during these two years was the way in which the process of acculturation had affected religious life in that church and many others. Religion was adapted to the mind-sets of our time and not really producing a Christian vitality at all. Nonetheless, I earnestly hoped that someday it would change. Upon completion of my comprehensive examinations, and personally fearing lest I be trapped into a teaching post somewhere, I opted to begin a regular pastoral ministry. It was my intention at that time to finish writing the dissertation and perhaps, much later in life, go back into a teaching post. After all these years I could now, as a fully ordained minister, preach the gospel of Jesus Christ and experience the marvelous fellowship of those who professed a like faith.

While my experience as a student pastor had been

somewhat restricting, I did feel that we could eventually discover a church of great beauty gathered about the name of Jesus.

Little did we know then the struggles that would evolve.

4

Church Experiences

It is love that asks, that seeks, that knocks, that finds, and that is faithful to what it finds. (St. Augustine)

The excitement of preparing for the ministry and the growing tendency in my mind to desire a vocation in a Presbyterian pulpit finally was realized when the two, small yoked churches invited us to become their pastor. They were situated in the lovely hills of northern New Jersey within driving distance of the seminary and it seemed that it would be possible for me to drive back and forth to complete my dissertation. At that point, I still had every intention of completing the doctorate. Nonetheless, my strongest desire was to begin to preach.

We were well received by these lovely people. They were gracious to their new, young pastor and his wife and eager to establish good relationships with us. They furnished the large manse which we loved so very much. They stocked the refrigerator with much good food to express their affection. We spent four marvelous years with them.

I recall many a night when I would drive back and forth to church and watch the changing moods come across the lovely countryside. I never drove home without a feeling of affinity for the beautiful, rural setting we were privileged to work in.

The church membership comprised a cross section of people, including farmers and professionals. Fresh out of seminary, with a strong evangelical thrust in my thinking, I longed to see the church become a beautiful, visible expression of the realities we found in Jesus Christ. The first hint that this might not be so came when we were installed. The visiting professor from Princeton Seminary who spoke at our installation leaned across the table at dinner and said to me: "Leonard, you do not have a church, you have a country club!" The remark registered at that time but really did not sink in until much later.

Soon after we arrived, some of the young married couples, who were very delightful people, approached us and said: "We, of course, do not wish to become fanatical in our faith!" While there is reasonableness in that statement, it also addresses a tragic lack in many churches of evangelical zeal to spread the message of Jesus Christ to our contemporary generation. Many of these young marrieds felt they had achieved something for God when they put on a steak dinner in order to raise money to "support the church." In fact, I became disturbed by what I called the "liturgy of church dinners and potluck suppers," particularly in light of the rather poor stewardship in giving.

Another puzzlement began to grow in my mind that the congregation was not really gospel-centered and Christ-centered! To be sure, they were believers. They would not think of expressing their faith in evangelical form for it was their conviction that one does not wear his religion on his coat sleeve. The congregation seemed, at least to my zealous, young, pastoral heart, far too passive and withdrawn from the focal point of a truly dynamic church.

Through the preaching of the gospel, careful exegesis of the Word of God, and the attempt to communicate the realities of Christ along with the excitement I felt belonged to those realities, I found myself facing insurmountable problems. How could I so communicate the message of Jesus as a Person, the Son of God, the Lord of the universe, the great Savior of mankind, the risen Christ at the right hand of the Father in such a way as to break through the facade of the people sitting in the congregation? How could I arouse them to action and relationships consistent with this kind of message? Often I felt like Don Quixote mounting his charger, putting his spear at his side, and deliberately charging the congregation with zeal. Just as the celebrated Quixote jousted with the windmill, and was thrown for a loss, so too did I eventually feel that my words were ricocheting off the minds and the hearts of my people. How could I communicate the genuine excitement and joy and love and power of the gospel?

I could not escape the thought that consistently

confronted me—if God depends on liturgical, sacramental, and institutional functions to confront the modern world, He is in great trouble! With powerful ideologies swirling about, communism capturing one half of the nations of the world, fascism and nazism having made powerful political and economic impacts upon modern times, the church seemed content to merely play at religion.

Intellectual and persistent questions could not be avoided. In the higher judicatories of our church we conducted business and yet I had the feeling that we were only verbalizing our internal problems. The thought frequently occurred to me that the only time we mentioned the name of Jesus was in a report or when we formally appended His name to a prayer. Why didn't the pastors, sensing the great needs both within the church and the environment, meet for extended intercessory prayer together? Our conversations were largely about church business, and we assumed the dedication and commitment of the other person. The schedule for business was so full that I never once recall the pastors and their elders going to their knees together for a prolonged period of real prayer. Apparently it was the job of the churches to conduct this kind of vital Christianity!

Meanwhile, I read continuously, seeking answers to the questions I could no longer escape. A church that has lost its evangelical fervor is bound to decline. Did not this cause great anxiety to those in administration? Was not the handwriting on the wall to be read by everyone?

I remember a conversation with a young pastor I had

instructed at Princeton, who later went on to achieve his doctor's degree and finally to pastor a very large and successful church. At a General Assembly meeting I asked him: "Bob, how would you evaluate the spiritual vitality of your church?" I will never forget the answer he gave: "Don't rock the boat!" I remember the discussion that followed as we talked about the need for compromise and political maneuvering within the church. The thought occurred to me that a pastor must be totally a man of God and sold out to the gospel of Christ and should not allow people to dictate to him the ultimate message that he feels God, in His divine call, has given him. A man of God must have the courage to follow the guidance of the living Christ and the Word of God if he is ultimately going to succeed in powerfully communicating the message of Christ.

A growing dissatisfaction increasingly gripped my heart. While I loved the people and appreciated their kindness, I nevertheless felt, from the standpoint of a Christian community, we lacked the spiritual and vital quality to reach our area as I felt we should. It was also clear that our people were not aroused to a joy in their personal faith and a strong desire to share the saving message of Jesus Christ.

Examination of other congregations and contact with other pastors revealed a pervasive sense of frustration in them also. Maybe the failure lay within myself, I wondered. Perhaps I was not really cut out to be a pastor of a growing and vital fellowship. Had I missed my calling? These thoughts, and others linked with them, depressed me. On the other hand, I began to consider if another situation would prove to be more productive and successful. Perhaps I should go back into teaching, finish my doctoral dissertation, and admit that I had made a wrong vocational choice. But why then was my longing to pastor and evangelize and teach in the local church situation so intense? The longing to succeed in the pastorate itself was always in my heart.

During this first pastorate our two wonderful children were born. Ronald Bruce and Carole Lynn are the names we gave to these two totally satisfying and rewarding children. Our congregation surrounded them with love and a sense of stability. They are both young adults now and they have told us that growing up in the manse was fun and filled with advantages and excitement. Our home was always full of interesting people, lots of laughter, and good times. The congregation became like a real family to us. Our children adopted the people as their grandmothers, grandfathers, aunts, uncles, sisters, and brothers. How grateful we are to them for their love. Nevertheless, I longed as well for a congregation excitingly committed to Jesus Christ and the gospel.

During our fourth year we received an invitation to pastor a large, inner city church which had a distinguished past. Many of our pastoral friends pleaded with us not to go in this direction, which they felt would be suicidal for our career in the ministry. The church had four pastors of considerable stature who had previously served it in the 104 years of its history. Its membership included men of great economic attainment. Substantial endowments ensured its longevity in spite of growing problems in racial interrelationships and the ghetto that was building around it. It not only had a prestigious past but it still had considerable strength. A fine choir, under able leadership, provided beautiful music. The people were largely devout and dedicated to their church. The previous pastorate, which had lasted thirty-two years under a very capable minister, had produced a faith that was genuine and a love for Christ and the church within the hearts of the people. In spite of these positive qualities, however, it was suffering the decline facing most inner city churches. They looked to leadership from their new pastor to reverse the disintegrating situation.

Perhaps, if we knew then what we have discovered more recently, things might have been considerably different. The strong evangelical flavor of our preaching, however, was not altogether acceptable to a few of the leaders. They felt they were being harassed—and perhaps they were. We had a dream, seemingly an unattainable dream, of a church that would exhibit those qualities of love and joy and excitement and powerful outreach that seemed to be the accompaniments of the early church. The inner city with its radical changes demanded a Christianity of immense power and practical magnetism. Programs were being devised in other inner city churches in the fond hope that the declining trend could perhaps be reversed. The area our church served was later to be torn by racial violence which was already smoldering in the neighborhood when we were there. Racial distrust was evident even in the church itself. The increasing black population sent their children to the church, but no amount of persuasion could attract the adults to the services in any great numbers. Beautiful choral presentations and excellent programs also failed to attract the population of the immediate area. It was quite apparent that we were not able to minister adequately to the changing sociological and economic needs of the area.

Why could not the church act as a healing, ameliorative, and uniting force? Certainly studies were made and great analyses were conducted. We were familiar with the problems and we commiserated together about them, but we could not seem to find helpful solutions. Why, with all of our resources, intelligence, and commitment, were we unable to find ways of reaching one another?

At that time—my own thinking which was solidly evangelical—was in itself inadequate to meet the needs of the area and even of the church. Somehow it seemed in my heart that if we could be adequately Christ-centered, by promoting the gospel, we could begin to affect our area and reach it and begin to see change. Every effort made in this direction seemed fated to failure or gross limitation. A tremendous sense of personal bankruptcy and of personal inadequacy invaded my own being. It wasn't just the church's problem, it was my own and that of other pastors in similar situations. Moreover, though the suburban churches seemed healthier in numbers, it was not convincing that they were any more spiritually vital or alive. Their sanctuaries were more full and their people more uniformly successful, but it appeared all too obvious that, in fact, the built-in inadequacies manifesting themselves in the city were quite clearly displayed in the suburban congregations as well.

Some strongly felt a liberal, humanistic approach was demanded; others insisted that the gospel was the answer and evangelicalism was the solution. Still others hoped a synthesis between the evangelical approach and social service would be found. Certainly prophets of the Old Testament and the writings of the New Testament emphasized considerable social concern. The liberal had caught something that was true to the mood of Scripture. On the other hand, the evangelical correctly insisted on a personal experience with Jesus Christ as being the solid foundation. Neither extreme alone seemed at this point to have adequate answers to the needs of our times. Certainly none that I could see were successful in resolving the black and white tensions made increasingly difficult by the Spanish-speaking who were moving into the same neighborhoods. Anger, fear, and anxiety increased in the ghetto.

Because of the seeming impassivity of the congregations to become vitally connected to Christ and to achieve the outreach that was needed, in my frustration I tended to become heavy-handed in the pulpit. My wife asked me a question over and over again: "How can you be such a normal person outside of the pulpit—filled with great sense of humor—and yet, when you mount the pulpit, become the apocalypse of doom?" She would irritate me by misquoting: "I am the bad shepherd, I beat my sheep!" At times she would tease me with parodies on songs such as: "I am so nervous in the service of the King!" Though happy at home, we were constantly looking for answers and reading voluminously for hidden keys.

One day I was visiting with an older, retired pastor from the inner city whose ministry was esteemed as eminently successful. I remember him saying, "So many years in the ministry; so little actually accomplished!" Why did Jesus promise so much and we realize so little? I could hear no answers except those that seemed like clichés in my mind. It became increasingly difficult to live in a bifurcated world where the secular and the sacred were separated. I somehow felt there would come an answer, that God would meet me down the way and something would happen.

My growing sense of frustration was turning to despair. I wanted to experience reality. I began to cry to God for help: "Either give me reality or give me death."

5

Search for Reality

Love can hope where reason would despair.
(George, Baron Lyttelton)

God had in some strange way shifted the burden and a certain sense of peace had come in. The intellectual struggle to find soluble answers was no longer the pressure. The prophet had said, "They that wait upon the Lord shall renew their strength" (Isa. 40:31). That waiting was a leaning back in the difficult and harsh circumstances of life's realities and waiting upon God's timing and God's solutions. Somehow I felt that, even though the situation was pretty much the same. The need remained as great as it ever was, the loneliness and intense hunger for undefined reality was still there, but the anxiety was somehow decreased. It was no longer simply my problem but also His!

We began to attend Faith-at-Work conferences. At these a man, by the name of Harold Hill, would sit for hours after the services and, with a crowd about him, share quietly what had taken place in his life as a former alcoholic who came to Christ. He not only told about his conversion but also about the divine healing power of the risen Christ. Could it be that the Lord Jesus was really mightily healing people today as He did when He walked upon the earth? That certainly was an exciting potentiality. One could not listen to Harold and deny the credibility of his witness.

This was, in fact, the first wedge into a new approach of life for me. A study of the Word reinforced the possibilities of this power being real for our days. Eagerly, I looked for anything I could find in the way of testimony and witness to the Lord's power to heal today. An Anglican minister from England shared the beauty of Christ's healing power that had flowed through him in the last twenty years. He explained how he had, in lonely fashion, instituted healing services in his church many years before. This was quite new in those days.

I felt as if I were being led! We were meeting people who supplied information which I had somehow overlooked before, all giving testimony and witness to Jesus' powerful actions in and through their lives. I was gripped with a tremendous feeling of excitement. To tell of Christ's present-day activities is far better than argumentative apologetics!

I will never forget those early days when in obedience we began to pray for the sick. Some people were healed; others apparently were not. This did not bother me too much at that time because I felt I was a child in

God's training school. Of course, as a Presbyterian, I knew about "His mysterious ways" and the lack of complete understanding did not disturb me all that much. Rather, I felt drawn adventurously into exploration.

Sometime during this searching period I encountered the book, *The Golden Sequence*, written by Evelyn Underhill. She had a chapter in it, as I recall, entitled, "The Purgation of the Intellect." This chapter argues that if we claim to know a great deal about Scripture and theology, it does not necessarily follow that we know much about the living God. It seemed to me that she was telling the reader to put all that knowledge aside and not to let it get in the way of a real contact with God. Others had tried to say the same in an attempt to unseat the orthodox from their simplistic answers and drive them to experience with God himself. I remember feeling a persuasion within that day, dropping to my knees, and simply saying to God, "Father, please teach me!" Again a strange consequence followed that prayer. There is a peace that overtakes the heart of a man who is willing to relax into God himself. It was as though I had taken off a heavy overcoat that had weighted me down for years. The strain of seeking answers was gone. A faith that He would meet me down the road seemed to pour into my being from somewhere. What a joy to be relieved of the necessity of providing all the answers myself! What a relief to acknowledge we don't have it all together! What freedom to the man who can honestly say, "I don't know." No longer defensive about any position, no longer seeking to have all the answers myself, I openly anticipated answers that would be in line with the Word of God and yet would possess a new quality of life.

One event which occurred around this time is yet strong in my mind. I had taken my wife to the A & P to purchase groceries while I stayed outside reading *Release* by Starr Daily. He describes a love relationship that gradually overtook him while he was a new Christian in prison. As he described his change of feelings toward his fellow-man, tears literally poured from my eyes to the point that I would have been embarrassed for anyone to see me. His beautiful story focused on the power of love and this shattered me.

Seated in my study one day and reading the biblical story of Jesus Christ going to Calvary, I felt a quality of His life and the beauty of His commitment gripping my heart. What moved me so much was not that He loved God, it was rather that He loved people! He loved them unto death. There was a strange and compelling beauty in Jesus Christ which I felt was connected to that simple fact. He was a man of great integrity and such beautiful simplicity and profound intelligence. His love for people was unconditional and he never selfishly preserved himself from the consequences of His commitments. I felt a terrible lack of a similar love within myself. Likewise, I sensed a corresponding lack of such expressed love in the church. I had been a Christian for many years and professed my faith in Christ. I had bent my mind to follow His teachings, as I understood them, and yet I sensed a great vacuum in my soul. How could a selfish man ever move to such a dimension of love? It seemed totally and psychologically impossible.

I recall the times when I would enviously read the writings of others who could express a love for Christ and reveal a beauty in character that I always felt was theirs by temperament and inheritance. How did one move from being *self*-centered to such outgoing love? Again the tears fell—for how long I will never know. All I do know is that my desk was soaked, as were my Bible and my clothes. Adoring the beauty and integrity of His person, the winsome juxtaposition of love and truth as I had never perceived them before, I fell to the floor of my study. With a heart filled with longing I simply cried: "Father, teach me to love my fellow-man as Jesus loved His fellow-man."

A series of prayers drawn from the heart of a spiritually bankrupt and broken pastor became the doorway to new life. "God, either give me death or give me reality." "Father, please teach me, for I do not have the answers; I cannot find my way." Finally, "Father, I cannot find you with all the intellectual searchings of my mind. Please teach me to find you with my heart. Teach me how to love my fellow-men as Jesus loved and loves His fellow-men."

I did not know that I was crying out to be filled and overwhelmed by His Holy Spirit. Though these were not my words theologically, our heavenly Father knows how to translate the cries of the human heart into the proper theological language!

Little did I realize the timing of God. Hundreds of thousands from every denomination were simultaneously and similarly crying to God for reality.

6

Hints of Reality

In the triangle of love between ourselves, God and other people, is found the secret of existence, and the best foretaste, I suspect, that we can have on earth of what heaven will be like. (Samuel M. Shoemaker)

My heartfelt prayers opened my mind and my heart to a profound reexamination and a potential discovery along lines other than the ones I had been exploring up to that point. Some keys came through reading, others through persons we met.

A lovely lady, Mrs. Sophie Panko, was one of these. As a housewife, she exhibited a loving, evangelical outreach and a demonstration of Christian reality that we had not seen up to that point. Her life touched the lives of literally hundreds of people with a singular beauty. Her witness for Jesus Christ and her apparent ease and joy with other people showed us the potential inherent in an individual life. At that time we did not understand that the secret of her life was love itself. We eventually hired her as church visitor and watched her lead many people to the Lord simply by serving their needs and sharing her loving witness.

We met others who would quietly share their personal faith, possessing a strange power to communicate the life and reality of Christ. These persons seemed remarkably gifted by God. Their openness and deep-seated joy radiated from their faces. What produced personalities that were so obviously alive and vibrant and exciting? I began to see bits and pieces of a huge puzzle in a disconnected way.

Then, for some strange reason, we began to hear amazing, incredible stories of healing brought about through prayer and intercession. Mr. Harold Hill had stunned my theological limitations when he suggested he had been miraculously healed of a ruptured disk in his back through the laying on of the hands of the evangelist, Oral Roberts. Could Jesus actually be healing through His body today in the same way that He did when He was on earth? I remember Dr. Emile Cailliet telling his class at Princeton Theological Seminary that Blaise Pascal had described with minute, scientific detail the miraculous healing of an eye disease through prayer. Unable at that time to handle such interventions of divine power, I simply filed it in the computer of my mind. Suddenly, credible witnesses everywhere were sharing quietly and unostentatiously the fact that Jesus had healed their bodies of various disturbances and illnesses.

My reexamination of the biblical accounts of healing certified that vast healing power certainly was manifested through Jesus and obviously carried on into the book of Acts. I no longer believed the argument that we now had the canon of Scripture ruling out the reality and necessity of God's healing power. Not only did Jesus himself heal—admittedly through the power of the Holy Spirit—but also the Christians of the early church were vehicles of healing through the divine name of Jesus. Moreover, these early Christians expected healing to be a fact (Acts 4). A careful examination of the whole New Testament gave me no negative instance or indication that this ministry of healing was ever to pass away. Encounters with the St. Luke Society, and pastors who had quietly been holding healing services in their churches, increased the excitement that was mounting within me. Fearfully, I began to pray for the sick, and saw beautiful evidences that the Word of God is self-validating when our faith is ready to believe.

At that point in our lives we were invited to the home of a Presbyterian elder in Summit, New Jersey. After a quiet evening of Bible study, while having tea with my host in one corner of the room, he pointed out three ladies who he said were quite remarkable. When I asked him why, he quietly shared that they had formed a prayer group among themselves and spent a great deal of time interceding for those who were sick and, he added very matter-of-factly, they were having remarkable results. I learned that all were in the teaching profession and two were members of the Christian and Missionary Alliance and one was a member of the Episcopal church. His next remark, however, was very unsettling. He simply stated, "And they often pray in the

Spirit!" It seemed that my mind was challenged by that assertion almost more than I wished. A certain aversion to the emotionalism believed to be contained within the Pentecostal movement almost caused me to turn away. Certainly this tradition could not offer anything to the vast intellectual research that we had been exposed to. Certainly this could not be the direction in which God was leading us. Nevertheless, the natural curiosity and inquiring questions could not be put aside. I simply had to ask those three ladies about their prayer for the sick, and they radiantly shared their joy in so praying. I then tentatively inquired about their "praying in the Spirit." In those days the charismatic experience had not largely invaded any of the mainline denominations.

They told of a hunger they had for more of the reality of Christ, a failure to be the kind of witness they desired to be, and a frustration about reaching goals they felt were implicitly biblical. They too, it seemed, had become aware of Jesus' power to heal in our day and had—as tentatively as myself—begun to pray for and to lay hands upon the sick in the name of Jesus. Very simply, they moved beyond healing to describe a growing awareness of their need for increased experience with and of the Holy Spirit and eventually to their coming into what they called the charismatic dimension. As they quietly shared their search and described eventually being, in their terms, "baptized in the Holy Spirit and speaking with another language," I found myself amazingly open to their witness. Perhaps their quiet demeanor and radiant faces and great honesty in communication gave me an inward peace to accept their words.

I now pursued a host of questions, largely along a specific line suggested by my own professor, Dr. Cailliet. He had asserted we should read the Scripture not simply to define theology but rather to ask the question what happened *in* the persons of the early church to enable these words to have been written. What actually happened to the people in the upper room at Pentecost for the words that described this event to be real? Could these same experiences be ours today? I was totally uninterested in the theological assertions that these things could not be for our day. A famous doctor at Johns Hopkins University who loved the Lord had said we must search for the existential realities that the Bible describes and not be prevented from these experiences by the theological explanations of those who would explain them away. Eagerly, I digested the whole book of Acts. Certainly something happened in the early church that was duplicated over and over again in the experience of the early Christians. They were filled with the Holy Spirit, they literally spoke in languages they had never learned. That was obvious. Now the declaration of the modern Pentecostals that they too were experiencing similar inward experiences with Christ could no longer be put aside as mere emotionalism. Moreover, I did not wish to do that.

Now the question arose: Why had this not been as focused in my attention before? Why had the church not placed the same emphasis upon the Holy Spirit that I now saw in the New Testament? Obviously we were not in balance with the Word of God. My studies of the gospels revealed that Jesus placed a strong and consistent emphasis upon the work and person of the Holy Spirit in His own life. He declared that His miracles were the evidence of the Spirit's work in Him. He emphasized that His teachings were transmitted to His heart and mind by the Father through the Holy Spirit. The emphases on the kingdom of God and the kingdom of heaven in the New Testament are indicative of the great power of the Holy Spirit operating through individuals and the corporate body of Jesus Christ. I sensed I was on the trail to a whole new world that had been in the Scriptures all along. I felt the bondage of traditional theology slipping off and a whole new world appearing.

I had always sought for security before, but now the new insecurity was more exciting than all the old securities had ever been. The sense of being led was more exciting and more fulfilling than the need for the theological positions I had previously taken. The promised land? I didn't know exactly what its contours would be, but the very facts of the recent encounters with others and Scripture reading and prayer and my spiritual hunger coalesced into a promise of fulfillment that was more exciting than anything I had previously known. Venturing with God and His promise of support was, as Kierkegaard pointed out, like swimming out over twenty thousand fathoms of water with a confidence that the hand of God was underneath and guiding.

7

Contact

*Divine love is a sacred flower, which in its early bud
is happiness and in its full bloom is heaven.*
(Eleanor Louisa Hervey)

My solitary and eager explorations of the New
Testament disclosed a world permeated by the reality of
the Holy Spirit. He totally resided in our Lord,
empowered the early disciples, inspired their speech,
and transformed their character. He was the mighty,
motivating force for their penetrating and successful
witness. The early church surged forward under His
direction.

I knew the "something that was missing" was here!
There could be no more question. He may have seemed
to the modern church, through lack of direct experience,
"the vague, oblong blur," yet His ministry in the
disciples was the unmistakable source for the power and
witness of their lives. Moreover this was clearly
emphasized throughout the New Testament. God's

anointing power came upon believers infusing their hearts with love for God and man, kindling their speech with persuasive power, and adorning their lives with moral integrity and beauty. This anointing clearly accounted for their profound level of commitment. Without controversy, we desperately needed to rediscover the person and ministry of the Holy Spirit, not in theology alone, but in life!

The Bible promised we could experience the powerful infilling of the same Holy Spirit who brooded over the chaos of primeval times, inspired the ancient prophets, indwelt our Lord in His incarnation, dynamically raised Him from the dead and supernaturally filled and moved the disciples. Even more, we were commanded by Paul to be filled with God's Holy Spirit! The obvious disparity between the supernatural landscape of reality in the Bible and our limited experience of the supernatural in modern life which had troubled me for years seemed bridged by the promise that I too could be "filled with His Spirit."

The brooding excitement of discovery prior to experience provoked discussion with several close pastor friends. They, in turn, became deeply interested. One of these, a Presbyterian pastor, decided on his own to attend Glad Tidings Tabernacle in New York City to observe and reconnoiter. This he did, expecting to hear a Pentecostal preacher. To his suprise, their guest preacher was a Presbyterian pastor, Dick Simmons, who was sharing how he experienced the promised Holy Spirit, paralleling the accounts in the book of Acts.

Following this service, my friend enquired of Dick

Simmons how we might learn more about the work of the Holy Spirit today. Dick told him that one of the finest expositors of the Word and of the life in the Holy Spirit was coming to the area and he would be available to speak to us. His name was David J. du Plessis, a Pentecostal preacher from South Africa who had been invited by Pope John to attend the Second Vatican Council.

The meeting was arranged and we invited a limited number of guests, including several clergy, to hear him. I was initially impressed by David's poise and quiet assurance. As he spoke for many hours from life and the Word of God, the Word literally leaped alive. His great love for the churches and their leaders, and his simplicity of interpretation of the gifts and the fruits of the Holy Spirit confirmed our earlier research.

That evening David spoke in a nearby Assemblies of God church. Desiring to hear more, we accompanied him. As he spoke of the outpouring of the Holy Spirit in our day my eyes filled with tears of longing. When an invitation was given for prayer and the laying on of hands we asked David to pray for us. His prayer for me was all too brief. With smiling eyes he assured me the Holy Spirit was within. I determined to pray the remainder of that night in the hope the Lord would manifest himself to me. To my disappointment no evidence happened—just great physical discomfort from prolonged contact with the floor.

A series of events after that brought the name of a Pastor Cooksey of Oyster Bay, Long Island, to my attention as one to whom I should speak. Through a phone call I obtained an invitation to spend the weekend at their small school. I shared my search with him and another fine pastor. They hospitably received me and surrounded me with prayer.

That Saturday, July 22, 1961, I intended to spend the day in prayer. Mr. Cooksey advised he would be busy that day, but would occasionally join me in prayer. Could he offer a suggestion? "Don't just pray—praise the Lord!"

So for many hours I alternately prayed, praised, and sang. Yet again nothing seemed to happen. So we went to dinner. Following dinner, I returned to the chapel to pray. About 9:00 P.M. Mr. Cooksey joined me, kneeling beside me at the simple platform. I was prayed out! This fine brother began to intercede for me with quiet fervor. I was deeply moved by his compassionate intercession. Then he prayed in tongues. The room was still. In English he spoke words to the effect: "My hand is heavy upon this man; he is very near." Whereupon I suddenly discovered myself quietly speaking a language we had not learned at the university or seminary.

There was no great emotion. It was as though my mind was analyzing this phenomenon. In fact, I was slightly disappointed by the lack of emotion. Pastor Cooksey was overjoyed.

Later that evening while I was lying on my bed a verse of Scripture seemed to pervade my whole being with a strange promise: "Ask of me, and I shall give thee the heathen for thine inheritance, and the uttermost parts of the earth for thy possession" (Ps. 2:8). Somehow I knew that God was changing my direction and would use my life for His glory.

The next day, Sunday, I discovered when I knelt to pray that I was praying again with a heavenly language. After the morning worship service I strongly felt I should return to my church in Newark.

Some time prior to these events someone had sent us a subscription to *Voice* Magazine, published by the Full Gospel Business Men's Fellowship. The stories contained in these little magazines never failed to touch my heart. I would read them with tears. I had written the Full Gospel Business Men's main office to thank them for the magazine and indicated I was searching. My letter was forwarded to Mr. Earl Prickett, an international director, who had held the letter for a long time desiring to come and visit me for the purpose of praying for me.

He was driving back to New Jersey from a Miami Full Gospel Business Men's convention in 1961 with his pastor and another Christian businessman. Though Earl had a business appointment with a large oil company, the three men felt led to visit me instead.

When they arrived at the Roseville Presbyterian Church the sexton told them I was away on vacation. They responded that I had to be there because God had led them to see me. He shrugged his shoulders at their strange insistence.

Meanwhile, still pondering the meaning of what had just taken place in my life and puzzled at why I felt I must remain at the church, I heard men's voices asking my secretary if they could speak with Pastor Evans.

As I looked across the long hall, one of the three strangers smilingly asked me if I knew who they were. I shall never forget the excitement as I assured them I did! I knew God had sent them! I just didn't know their names.

Earl Prickett informed me he had received my letter from the F.G.B.M.F.I. office, and they had come to pray for me that I might be filled with the Holy Spirit! It was a joy for me to share my news—the Lord had already answered their prayers! That night I experienced a depth of Christian fellowship with these three men I had never experienced before.

8

The Agony and the Ecstasy

Faith, like light, should always be simple and unbending; while love, like warmth, should beam forth on every side, and bend to every necessity of our brethren. (Martin Luther)

As my three new friends, Earl Prickett, Anthony Calvanico, and A.C. Sorelle, shared their stories and told me about the new, exciting fellowships of hungry men congregating together, it seemed I had a glimpse of the promised land. Men who loved the body of Christ, and sought intensively for her resurgent vitality, were everywhere about me. The book of Acts was not an antique representation of a moment of excitement in the early church's history, but was being reproduced in a marvelous and historic way in the hearts of men and women everywhere.

Soon invitations to speak across the United States and Canada poured in. Thousands of people congregated at great conventions to hear the witness of others describe how God had caused them through desperate search to discover the dynamic of the Holy Spirit. I spoke in some of those great conventions with a sense of participation in an historic moment in the economy of God. Peter could not have been more excited in discovering Cornelius than we were in discovering each other. The fellowship experiences were satisfying in a way almost totally unknown in the organized churches. The sense of *koinonia* in prayer and adventure of witness was outstanding. How thrilling to meet laymen and ministers and priests whose whole lives were consumed with a passion for the kingdom of God: Glorious meetings were followed by long discussions as men and women sensed they were part of a marvelous move of God. Tears of love and joy flowed easily and radiant faces lit up with the potentialities that God was placing in our hands. The shared joy in these meetings, on the one hand, and the church-as-usual routines, on the other, revealed a sharp and disappointing contrast. If only the people sitting in the pews could participate in meetings where God was intensely found and worshiped, would they not desire the same thing for themselves?

For many years I had preached the gospel of Jesus Christ in the fond hope that many would turn to Him and be revolutionized by His indwelling presence. What happened, rather, was an assimilation of the truth into what seemed to me placid and innocuous states of commitment. Our worship lacked joy and sought traditional dignity. Our people had not previously responded to the message of God's great saving plan to reach the world; likewise, they did not respond to our preaching on the power and work of the person of the Holy Spirit. I shared joyously what had taken place in my life. To my surprise and consternation things did not greatly change. The people seemed content to remain as they were. Tradition seemed to satisfy them. The more I struggled to communicate my new found joy the less it seemed they were willing to listen.

Even my wife seemed disinterested and unresponsive. Although we had always had a good relationship, I felt misunderstood and I thought perhaps she felt I was on a new mystical tangent. She later explained to me that she had felt alienated in terms of this new experience and my joy in my new friends. This was strange because for all our lives we had walked together in a gentle understanding. I interpreted her feelings as criticism and became increasingly defensive. A sense of uneasiness began to invade my mind. To be sure, as I was invited to speak at these great conventions of hungry people, I always felt great satisfaction and excitement. But always I had to go home. The more I preached the gospel and added the dimension of the infilling of the Holy Spirit, the more it seemed I felt alone. Was my life always going to be so unsettled? The joy and happiness persisted inside but the environment was not as adaptable to change or to the realization of my great dreams as I had fondly hoped. The congregation became confused regarding my expectations and quietly dug in their heels.

Once again I thought of changing pastorates. Perhaps we could find a fellowship that shared my excitements, my dreams, my anticipations. But where was such a church?

I was beginning to develop a certain philosophy about prayer. That is, God can make one miserable in one of two ways: either He can say no to our prayers or yes to our prayers! It seemed to me He always said yes to mine, for in some way I would always ask for the wrong thing. Nonetheless, I believed that a change was necessary.

Our very dearest friends from the church we served in Newark had moved to Alexandria, Virginia. We planned to visit them early in the week. Just prior to this visit we received a communication from the Washington Presbytery informing us that they had examined hundreds of dossiers of pastors and had selected mine to be considered for a new church in the area surrounding Washington, D.C. It would become a very important church and they wanted eagerly to meet us. This coincided with our visit to our friends and we thought perhaps this was the direction of the Holy Spirit.

We met with our friends and they and my wife sought to persuade me not to share with the presbyter and others about my experience with the Holy Spirit, for they assured me that this would foreclose any possibility of receiving the call. Disliking deceit of any kind, I reluctantly consented not to initiate such a conversation. With the presbyter, we circled the whole Washington, D.C. area including both Maryland and Virginia and he pointed out the growing population of this vicinity. We shared mutually our faith and our desires. We met at lunch with some of the pastors of the presbytery and they seemed open and agreeable to our coming. At the end of a long day—having seen the area where the new church would begin and having satisfactorily answered all of the presbyter's questions—we returned to the National Presbyterian Church for a moment of conversation with a second presbyter. We were introduced to the latter enthusiastically and excitedly as our friend of the day shared how he was deeply impressed with my personality and commitment and the way I "exhibited more enthusiasm for the gospel than anyone he had ever met." He felt, in fact, that I was the man for the position.

But quietly the other presbyter, a fine returned missionary, broached a new subject. He asked me, as he reviewed my dossier, "I see, Mr. Evans, that you are interested in spiritual healing." He then went on to ask if I was familiar with the new charismatic movement that was taking place in our country. I shared with him how I had received the infilling of the Holy Spirit. How grateful I was that this was brought out into the open. I shared with him some of my recent experiences. Immediately we knew that this door was closed! The other presbyter looked crestfallen. He said sympathetically, "Leonard, I do believe that your experience would make you too controversial a person to put in a new Presbyterian church. Perhaps an older church, but certainly not a new one." I immediately sensed my wife's disappointment. She had already seen the new manse. It was gorgeous, situated in a high income area and beautifully appointed with French provincial furniture.

Wondering if my new experience in the Holy Spirit might prevent any ministerial committee from looking with favor upon our transfer to another parish, upon our return I entered the sanctuary of the large Roseville Presbyterian Church and knelt at the platform looking up at the beautiful Tiffany window, my favorite place to pray. Simply, I asked God if there might be a church somewhere that could use the man that I had become. In the early 1960s, as the charismatic movement was beginning, the churches did not know how to receive or even how to handle such as I was. Feeling that even this would present quite a problem to God, I nonetheless had peace. I had decided long ago not to hide or play the diplomatic game. If the Holy Spirit was, as we were to discover, the Spirit of love, He is at the same time the Spirit of absolute, transparent integrity and honesty. Though I could not foresee the direction that might come and was a bit anxious concerning my relationship with my beloved Presbyterian church, I nonetheless waited upon God.

My own presbytery and my fellow Presbyterian pastors were always kind and understanding. Perhaps they thought I'd become a bit of a speckled bird, but they never treated me with any great distance. They did look a little askance when I shared with them what had taken place in my life. I wondered if perhaps I might have to venture in a new direction. Could I search out new forms of worship within the Presbyterian church without countering some of the longstanding traditions? I did not wish to unsettle anyone or to cause any grief. I wondered if perhaps I should search for a pastorate outside the bounds of the presbytery where we could more freely experiment with new forms of relationship and new forms of worship.

9

Unfulfilled Promise

*Faith has to do with the basis, the ground on which
we stand. Hope is reaching out for something to
come. Love is just being there and acting.* (Emil
Brunner)

They looked like and acted like a pulpit committee,
but they never said they were. They'd come from the
Islington Evangel Centre in Toronto, Canada,
ostensibly to visit a friend whom they loved in the Lord.
We had met these wonderful people on previous trips to
Toronto for speaking engagements. It was a small
church they represented but the people seemed
dedicated to the Lord Jesus and experienced in the
work of the Holy Spirit. Our visit with the men that
evening was extremely pleasant. They did say they were
looking for a pastor and had been visiting a church in
another area of New Jersey. They gave no indication,
however, that they were at all interested in calling me.
They later shared they felt we would not be interested in
pastoring their small assembly.

After they left, a long-distance phone call came from Toronto and again my friends shared their concern to find just the right man. We assured them of our deep and committed prayer on their behalf, whereupon they asked if we would consider a call from them. I felt that maybe this was God's direction. Bette was not eager to go to a charismatic church for she was not convinced of the charismatic experience. But feeling that perhaps it would make me finally happy and perhaps lead to the realization of our long dream, she consented.

The church was independent, unconnected with any denomination. We presented the call to the presbytery and requested permission to labor "outside the bounds of presbytery." Reluctantly and with much love, our fellow presbyters commended us to our new adventure, consenting to our request for this particular relationship. I shall always appreciate the support and love and consideration shown me by my colleagues. I had to follow what Socrates called the "inner guidance system." I had to pursue my quest.

When visas had been obtained and our Volkswagen was six months old (to avoid high customs tax) we moved to Toronto and to our new Canadian parish. Church board meetings in our new pastorate often began with extended periods of prayer together on our knees. Their sincerity and expectancy spoke to my heart. They too wanted to see the Holy Spirit move in greater power. They believed that their educated, Spirit-filled Presbyterian pastor would be a signal key. Was he not already traveling across North America speaking and would not God greatly bless his ministry?

Moreover, some of them were leaders in the Full Gospel Business Men's Fellowship and they would share traveling with us and the joys of speaking to fellow Christians.

Worship experiences were extremely beautiful and the singing was exquisite beyond description. How marvelous to be part of a congregation that expected miracles and believed in the activities and the gift ministries of the Holy Spirit. They believed unequivocally in the power of Jesus to heal today. Our beginnings were filled with joyous expectations. No longer did we feel any sense of holding back from any segment of the congregation. There seemed to be a marvelous unity of purpose and direction.

Certain problems eventually did manifest themselves, however, in a very puzzling way. Though they believed in the power of Jesus to heal, many were quite ill. Neither were they quite as evangelically efficient as we had somehow expected. The church had been small in its beginnings and had remained relatively small for a number of years.

It is one thing to experience a deep sense of love and power in great conventions and retreats; it is quite another to learn to love one another over extended periods at the local church level. Is it that we know each other too well? Is it that we become aware of the rather evident limits and weaknesses we all have?

At any rate, it soon became apparent that we had not yet reached Utopia. Reluctantly, we faced still extremely persistent questions. Did not Paul say that the gospel was the power of God unto salvation? We saw here, as we had in earlier congregations, the gospel reach into the hearts of men and women from time to time. We did see evidence of His presence, but the promised fruitfulness of John 15 was still not as evident as we believed it should be. The people looked for and enjoyed tremendously the mighty experiences that attended beautiful and deeply satisfying worship. They seemed, at least to me, to strain toward ever increasing mystical experiences with Christ. They yearned for a greater manifestation of the gift ministries of the Holy Spirit.

Although we prayed and served sincerely, things were not happening quite as we had expected. They indeed loved us deeply and prayed for us intensely, but I sensed in their attitudes the implication: "Pastor, we know that you've been filled with the Holy Spirit, but you leak!" and that's exactly how I felt. It had always been a strain for me to try to achieve the kind of spirituality I had been led to expect. I knew that I leaked from every pore! The more I struggled to be intensely spiritual the less it actually took place. I too wanted to see the mighty manifestations of the Holy Spirit in healing. I longed with them to see the mighty gift ministries of the Spirit in operation. Nevertheless, I had to conclude they were not taking place. Yes, there was an occasional speaking in tongues and interpretation, but even these did not seem always too exciting. They seemed somewhat repetitious. I wondered at times if God was not afflicted with cliches. Certainly there had to be more.

Being a masochist by nature, I felt perhaps the problem was within me. In intense and sincere prayer I asked God to teach me how to love Him more realistically and more deeply. I literally yearned for the great outpouring of the Holy Spirit in our midst. But weeks, months, and even years followed—our expectations were still not attained. How many times I cried, "Oh God, enlarge my heart to love you more!" If nothing else I was extremely sincere. I yearned for these people to experience all they hungered for.

Not that they did not try to help me. Lovingly, they took me to hear "anointed" ministries in, I believe, the fond hope that something would wear off on their pastor. Many looked longingly to the ministries of others whose national attention was gained through healing ministries. Why did we not see these great healing manifestations take place in our church?

Internal frustration forced me to ask myself whether I must always be a searcher and never one who actually finds. To be sure, there are always goals ahead and achievements to be accomplished. Nor could I help noticing that many in our congregation looked backward to former times of great experiences with God.

I loved them so much that my wrestling with God became increasingly intense. They prayed for my anointing. I prayed for their satisfactions. I was still searching! I pored over the whole Bible looking for further answers and, in particular, intensely studied the Old Testament prophets. It was remarkable to me how much they talked about human relationships. One could not read Amos or Jeremiah or Isaiah or the minor prophets without sensing a practicality of message. The prophets seemed concerned with justice, mercy, and truth. We seemed to be looking for ever increasing and intensely satisfying mystical experiences. There were vast hungers for gift ministries, but not always a corresponding hunger for practical, loving relationships with each other. I sensed, as I continued reading, a growing divergence from the expectancies of our people. Reluctantly and yet compellingly, I pursued the clues of the Old Testament.

Were we expecting too much at the level of mystical experience? How does all this equate with the thrust of Scripture which concerns itself largely with man's relationship to his fellow-man. The vertical relationship with God is admittedly extremely important, but it seemed we paid insufficient attention to the person-to-person relationships I increasingly saw once again to be the main thrust of Scripture. I, at least, had to conclude that much of my search for deeper mystical experience had been frustrating across the years. Paul suggests that we should be filled with God's Holy Spirit. What does it really mean to be "filled with the Holy Spirit"? It had to be more than an intense religious experience! The very context of Ephesians, chapter 5, dealt again with relationships and not primarily mystical experiences as such. Actually, I was beginning to see that this intense desire for religious experiences often drove healthy people away. They felt perhaps we had found something, but their inner Geiger counters gave them a sense of uneasiness in our presence. Likewise, religious expression is not universally appealing. Moreover, the desire for further mystical experience drained people rather than satisfying them.

Meanwhile, I continued reading much in the gospels and the epistles and saw again the practical emphases of the whole Bible. A dear friend of mine in the church in Islington, a fine businessman, would say to me over and over again, "Pastor, how will all this that we're accenting in the church on Sunday help me Monday morning at the office?" He and several others were beginning to ask penetrating questions.

All my life I had been conditioned by my religious training to believe in ever-increasing and ever-intensifying relationships with God! The standards and calculations by which we measured growth were the experiences we felt we should continually have in His presence. The evangelical tradition had largely avoided the humanitarian questions raised by the liberals, and so had retired into an explicitly spiritual linguistic statement. Yet I could not fail to see the relational characteristics of much or most of the language of Scripture. Again Ephesians 5 expressed our Christianity in terms of basic human relationships of marriage, family, and vocation. Obviously, to be filled with the Holy Spirit had to affect these very practical relationships.

Ephesians 5:18 constantly was in my mind. "Be filled with the Spirit!" What did it mean to be filled with the Holy Spirit? And if I were filled with His Spirit, how would I feel inside?

Again my training had led me to look for increased and intensified relationships with God, fortified by prayer and by the sacraments and by worship

71

experiences. But how did one carry this into the routines of daily life? Certainly the Pauline epistles dealt largely with questions of character and conduct. The miraculous and supernatural landscape of reality was quite apparent in the gospels and the book of Acts and throughout the epistles. But I began to sense the average New Testament citizen lived a fairly normal and routine life, illuminated by his faith and cherished in his relationships. Frequently the invading power of the Holy Spirit was manifest and should be today as well. A reading of Paul's letter to the Philippians, particularly chapter one, revealed very clearly that Paul shared the same limitations we do. He was not certain of his future destiny in history. He was certain about his Lord, but he was uncertain about the exact path that lay ahead. He shared that in common with me. He knew times when his friends were not healed as he advised Timothy to take a little wine for his stomach's sake and thanked God for sparing Epaphroditus from near death. It was not always a supernaturalistic movement but a natural joy in relationships.

One day, while standing in the pulpit, several questions would not leave my mind during our time of worship. Very quietly, I turned to God and addressed them to Him: "Father, what does it mean to be filled with your Holy Spirit? How would I feel if I were literally filled with your Spirit? What would my behavioral characteristics be if I were filled with your Holy Spirit? What would a church really look like if it were filled with your Holy Spirit? How would marriage be if we were literally filled with your Holy Spirit? Why do all of these areas exhibit so much unfulfillment even among those of us who call ourselves Spirit-filled? God, there has to be something more implicit within this experience that we are not yet clearly seeing. Please teach me!"

10

Simplicity:
the Love Message of Jesus

*Beloved, let us love one another: for love is of
God; and every one that loveth is born of God,
and knoweth God.* (1 John 4:7)

What would a church look like that exhibited the
characteristics of being filled with the very Spirit of
almighty God? I knew that the answers I might find
would be valid historically, psychologically, and
biblically and have deep and abiding value for the whole
body of Christ. I knew my search was more than
personal and would be corporately significant. The
Bible had provided the key for the mighty Reformation
in Luther's day; it was certainly capable as the Word of
God to inspire answers adequate for our own time and
need.

One day I turned to 1 John 1. As I pondered this
beautiful chapter over and over again several thoughts
leaped electrifyingly from the pages. John was
reminiscing about his early days as a young man in the

75

presence of Jesus. They had actually seen the Word of life, had heard Him with their ears, had looked upon Him with their eyes and had touched Him with their hands and had bivouacked with Him upon the hillsides at night. What must it have been like to see the face that had never known guile or spoken deceit? How I envied young John that early experience. Now the older man was looking back reflectively upon it. He was reminiscing about the marvel of it, exploring the wonder of it in his soul. They had actually contacted the living Son of God who had created the worlds as the agent of the Father. But one verse suddenly struck a strange note within:

> That which we have seen and heard declare we unto you, that ye also may have fellowship with us: and truly our fellowship is with the Father, and with his Son Jesus Christ. (1 John 1:3)

This verse reflected an awareness of the presence of the Father and the Son no doubt through the experiential reality of the Spirit in a way that I still felt was strange to our modern day experience. We, who fellowship and worship together in the modern church, would say doctrinally the same thing, but we have been so literally unconvincing that the world has not beaten a path to our door. To say that the living God is literally in our midst and not just sacramentally present or poetically present is extremely exciting. Certainly worship should be deeply infected with this awareness. Why did it not seem to be as realistic to us as it was to them? These thoughts were excitingly present in my mind. What secret did they possess which we appear not to have?

Another verse was nearly as exciting. "This then is the message which we have heard of him, and declare unto you, that God is light, and in him is no darkness at all" (1 John 1:5). Light and dark—light versus the dark! I had always been intrigued by John 1:4 which says, "In him was life; and the life was the light of men." For some reason "light" had always suggested to my mind theological completion and comprehension, the great intellectual truths and realities about our faith; "the dark" was confusion and lack of such understanding. But "light" seemed to have a different connotation in 1 John. I noticed that John moved from light to love and dark to hate. Again, these terms were descriptive of inner moral attitudes and corresponding personal and ethical or non-ethical relationships. I noticed that John said, "He that loveth his brother abideth in the light, and there is none occasion of stumbling in him. But he that hateth his brother is in darkness, and walketh in darkness" (1 John 2:10, 11). Obviously this was again emphasizing relationships as being critically vital.

I saw something beautiful about our heavenly Father. There was no darkness at all in Him; *He was explicitly light!* I saw that if one could translate "light" as "love," as John seemed to do, a whole new landscape would emerge. John was later to write, "Beloved, let us love one another: for love is of God; and everyone that loveth is born of God, and knoweth God. He that loveth not knoweth not God; for God is love" (1 John 4:7, 8).

What a beautiful revelation of my heavenly Father! He knows and experiences none of the ugly and vicious and destructive things that so contaminate human nature. *He is pure love!* No wonder Jesus could say, "Him that cometh to me I will in no wise cast out" (John 6:37). Love cannot be other than it is; it may know anger at sin, but it can never know hate toward persons for it would then submerge itself in our own violations. No matter where I touched Him I discovered God is love! He will never turn against me, He is always for me, never against me. He did not send His Son into the world to condemn us but to bring us to life, to love, to joy, to happiness, and to interpersonal relationships that were manifestly of that same order and character.

It was stated so clearly: "If we walk in the light [and I am persuaded that "light" is the correspondent analogy for "love"], as he is in the light, we have fellowship *one with another,* and the blood of Jesus Christ his Son cleanseth us from all sin" (1 John 1:7). When does He promise to cleanse us from sin? As we walk in the love that is placed within our hearts for each other by the Holy Spirit, we are in a state of constantly being cleansed by the efficacious work of His blood and the resulting presence of the Holy Spirit. It seemed to me that the goal and purpose of God in salvation was to bring us to this state of interpersonal love.

Mighty thoughts began to surge through my mind. There are too many for this single book. In a subsequent book I hope to develop the theology and ontology that lies behind the love commandment of Jesus Christ. In a second work I hope to develop the marvelous and adventurous and exciting simplicity that lies behind Jesus' single commandment to His people: "A new commandment I give unto you, That ye love one another; as I have loved you" (John 13:34).

It seemed that all of Scripture suddenly came flamingly alive. But it was a single verse that was ultimately to revolutionize my whole approach to the Christian walk. "Seeing ye have purified your souls in obeying the truth through the Spirit unto unfeigned [non-hypocritical, genuine, sincere, true, real] love of the brethren, see that ye love one another with a pure heart fervently" (1 Pet. 1:22).

Had that Scripture been in the Bible all these years? Why had I not seen it before in the way I was seeing it this day? It seemed to me that this verse was saying that we were born again and filled with the Spirit not so much to love God as to have God's love created in us for one another, that the purpose of our salvation was not so much to throw our love back to the Father as it was to receive His love and extend it to our fellow-man. It seemed eminently practical and inviting and suggestive of whole new areas of exploration and adventure.

I discovered several things were wrong with my own personal life immediately. All my life I had seen that God was a God of love. Ravished by that love personally and having experienced it through Jesus Christ, I made the mistake of trying to throw that love back to God himself. It seemed to me that was my highest office and most sincere response. But it was not what Scripture dictated. I suddenly realized that God was like an infinite reservoir of love, a faucet pouring forth love indiscriminately upon His sons and His enemies alike. God *is* love; He does not merely *have* love! Ravished as I was by that love, I wanted to reaffirm my love for Him constantly and so I connected the hose of my life to that faucet that I might draw His love within my heart and mind and soul, but I had made a great mistake. I sought to send the water back to the faucet! I suddenly realized no hose works that way. One connects the hose to the faucet to receive the life-giving liquid and then transmits it to the garden that the flowers, plants, and vegetables might grow.

I heard again in my heart those great parallelisms of Scripture: "As I have loved you, that ye also love one another" (John 13:34). "If I then, your Lord and Master, have washed your feet; ye also ought to wash one another's feet" (John 13:14). "As the Father hath loved me, so have I loved you: continue ye in my love" (John 15:9).

What a fool I have been all my life. Driven by the compulsion for a deeper walk with God and a more mystical and satisfying experience with Him, I had forfeited that result by not seeing this simple truth. How mistaken I was. Could this be why the churches did not reflect that radiancy and glory and power that could attract a hungry world to the message God had given to it? The church I knew then did not seem to exhibit either to itself or to the world that quality of radiant, interpersonal love that cannot fail to draw men to the Christ it serves. They had pointed vertically to the love of God and the love commended from God to man, but they had frustrated that same message by a failure to joyously exhibit the self-accepting and other-accepting love that could have been so attractive to men morassed in persistent failure. What would a church really look like that actually lived out this love as it preached its message of God's love? That question intrigued me. Could such a church actually be brought into being? Could a congregation so manifest this love that people would be attracted, as I felt they would, by the thousands? Could Christians overcome their differences and polarizations and hostilities under the inspiration of the Spirit to actually demonstrate this missing quality?

The whole New Testament seemed replete with similar indications. All of them came glowingly alive to me. For instance, *"And the Lord make you to increase and abound in love one toward another, and toward all men, even as we do toward you: To the end he may stablish your hearts unblameable in holiness before God, even our Father, at the coming of our Lord Jesus Christ with all his saints"* (1 Thess. 3:12, 13). Why had these verses been submerged in the text for so long?

In effect, Paul is saying, "May the Lord himself cause you—work upon you, run the hands and fingers of His love up and down your heart—to increase more and more and more and more to the point of overabounding in love *one toward another and toward all men* even as we demonstratively do toward you." It became so apparent again to me that the result of receiving God's love was not to return it so much to God or even to Christ as it was to pass it in unbounded measure to others. That was why salvation came, that was the goal adequate to a Pentecost of the New Testament.

The great hunger for some mystical interpenetration into God may be satisfying to a few, but I sensed it was not practically satisfying to the majority. Perhaps some do venture deep within the cavernous centers of the great cathedrals of faith, but the great majority stand at the door with Sam Shoemaker seeking satisfying interpersonal relationships and seeking to acquaint men with the simple love of God. Once again I noted: "We love him, because he first loved us" (1 John 4:19). The King James Version translates it "we love *him*" (signifying God), but most other translations agree that the word "him" does not appear in the original. We love each other and we love our fellow-man because we have been quickened and empowered by the irradiating love of God who is a pure flame of love for His creature, man. John 3:16 cannot be explained in any way other than this: God is a passionate lover of His creature, man. The gift of His Son through the incarnation and His passionate atonement can only describe a love beyond human calculation. No wonder His selfless love sought not a return of love so much as an expression of love to Him through others.

Further along in the gospel of John the same message is illustrated again (John 15). As Jesus describes himself as "the true vine" and His Father as "the husbandman" and every branch abiding in Him bearing fruit or not bearing fruit with consequent purgation or severance, our thoughts normally turn to a devotional type of life and an increase in devotion to God. Advised to abide in Jesus, I had sought an ever-increasing, intense prayer relationship with Him that I might feel close to Him. With great promise He had assured His followers that if His words and He himself did abide in them, they would have magnificent and effectual power in prayer. I was commended by the pulpit to seek the face of God in ever-increasing intensity of prayer which is so desirable, of course. Nonetheless, the whole message of Jesus was made ambiguous to me by the religious teachings of my past and darkened by the expectancies I was falsely led to develop.

"As the Father hath loved me, so have I loved you: continue ye in my love. If ye keep my commandments, ye shall abide in my love; even as I have kept my Father's commandments, and abide in his love. These things have I spoken unto you, that my joy might remain in you, and that your joy might be full. *This is my commandment, That ye love one another, as I have loved you*" (John 15:9-12). These words leaped alive to me.

There it was again so clear, so unmistakable, so obvious that I believe we've missed it down through the ages. We have pursued intricate theological constructions, deep and intellectual persuasions, but we have not just obeyed this simple injunction which would have led to discoveries far exceeding the greatest theological formulas. Why did many who obviously profess love for Jesus Christ and who as obviously do love Him fail to exhibit the simple qualities these verses indicate? Where was this great love? We had seen tokens of it in the local churches and small indicators of its presence, but the overwhelming sense of love it described we had not seen adequately demonstrated anywhere. To be sure, the great conventions of Spirit-filled believers demonstrated this to an unusual degree. But I had not seen it at that time translated into the life of the church. Moreover, I had seen, conversely, division and separation and hostility and competition even among those who claimed the full gospel message. Obviously, this simple commandment yet lay beyond the experience of a good many of us. Yet its message was plain, at least to my heart and my soul.

Jesus knew that His disciples loved Him and He advanced the way they could demonstrate that love to Him and prove their deep affection for Him. If they loved Him they would keep His commandments! How many commandments were there? There were ten in the Old Covenant and all of us have failed dismally to fulfill these! What were His commandments? He never leaves us in the dark.

The Lord answers this question forthrightly: *"This is my commandment,* That ye love one another, as I have loved you" (John 15:12). Very explicit direction. It was a command and not a suggestion.

I later discovered in the book of Deuteronomy, that great Old Testament Book of the Law, that the way in which we express our affection for God is to obediently do what He asks us to do. And always in Deuteronomy He shows that we would cleave unto Him if we kept His commandments and His exhortations! And these were to walk in justice and love and mercy, as Micah had said, with our fellow-man (Mic. 6:8).

Moreover, there would be *joy* if we would so love. Does not the fruit of the Spirit indicate this in Galatians

5:22, 23? The fruit of the Spirit was, as Paul so clearly stated, *love!* *Love* that brought in its train peace, that produced a pervasive joy; *love* that was longsuffering in character; *love* that was gentle and kind; *love* that had a basic goodness implicit in its faith; *love* that had fidelity to its fellow-man at the very center of its life; *love* that had a basic humility and meekness and self-control against which there was no law indeed. *Love!*

To be sure, many had read these words and even in a sense understood them. The only thing lacking was a fulfillment and a childlike obedience. Why did we not as Christians take that crystal clear commandment of our Lord Jesus to heart as sincerely as we fought and argued and discussed our varieties of religious understanding? Why did we not lay down our lives for our brother? Why was gross selfishness so obviously still present in so many of our lives—even those who claimed to be "Spirit-filled"? It was apparent at least to me that we in the church who profess the name of Christ did not take seriously this commandment to heart. If we had, I knew our churches would be packed to the doors with those enquiring and seeking after what we had found. I knew that it was more than just professing the gospel of Christ that was needed in our world. I knew that men would not be satisfied by pure orthodoxy of expression but needed a practical Christianity demonstrated before them. It was so obvious and clear that where this did in fact exist, a joy would be so present that people would wonder at its source. A noted Roman Catholic philosopher and theologian has said that joy would be the infallible sign of the presence of the living God. I knew immediately that if a church or congregation or fellowship could discover this among themselves and literally persevere in the the performance of love and commitment to each other, such a fellowship or congregation inevitably would grow in effectiveness, outreach and impact.

Bell Telephone has a saying, "Let your fingers do the walking!" Literally, my fingers ran through the whole of the New Testament and the Old Testament and everywhere I turned I discovered the same message. Imagine my joy at discovering John 14 and the ontology that lies behind the love commandment of Jesus Christ. Always I had longed to feel consummately close to the Lord. I knew we did not live by feelings, but when one is devoid of them for great lengths of time and devoid of that presence of joy as is promised, the going gets hard. Also that longing to feel encased in the Father's love persisted. How could I find it?

Suddenly I saw how it all came together.

> He that hath my commandments, and keepeth them, he it is that loveth me: and he that loveth me shall be loved of my Father, and I will love him, and will manifest myself to him. Judas saith unto him, not Iscariot, Lord, how is it that thou wilt manifest thyself unto us, and not unto the world? Jesus answered and said unto him, If a man love me, he will keep my words: and my Father will love him, and he will come unto him, and make our abode with him. (John 14:21-23)

All that my heart had longed for was clearly promised in this simple statement. I had yearned across the years to feel close to God, but He had unfortunately hidden himself in the one place I was not seriously looking for Him—He was sitting at my kitchen table! He lived and moved and had His being in my wife and children. I had always loved them and considered them my fellow Christians, but I had hungered for something more. Suddenly I saw that everything I longed for was seated at my kitchen table. All I had to do was to love Bette with the same intensity that God had loved me and I would have felt the overwhelming sense of His presence! All a congregation has to do is to pour the same love out to others that they have received from God and they likewise would sense and feel the power and the presence of the living God! What a fool I had been in my personal life. How I had short-changed my dear wife by all of my religious and mystical hungers. God had never intended them to be as I understood them. He sought rather to satisfy me and to produce in me a joy in living that I had never really found. By extension I knew the same was true for the church of the living Christ. No discoverer of continents or mining engineer tapping into a rich vein of precious ore could have felt one-half the excitement I felt as this message began to focus together before my eyes. Utterly simple, exquisitely practical—I knew that I had stumbled onto the mind of Jesus Christ!

11

Mercy not Sacrifice: the Narrow Way

Love is the doorway through which the human soul passes from selfishness to service and from solitude to kinship with all mankind. (Anonymous)

How paradoxical to my former theology was that discovery. The closer I drew to Bette in love and service, the nearer God promised to draw to me! Then I discovered Colossians 3. Here Paul exhorts believers to seek those things which are above, where Christ sits on the right hand of God, if we are indeed risen with Christ. We are encouraged to set our affection on things above, not on things on the earth.

At first glance this seems to support that deep mystical approach which had been fraught with such bitter disappointment in my life. "Above" seemed to have the quality of other-worldliness, perhaps even intense inwardness. I remember saying to myself, in argument with Paul, that if what so many thought he was saying was true, then perhaps Karl Marx was right in criticizing

Christians for seeking "pie-in-the-sky-bye-and-bye." Were we not so often accused of a major cop-out in the interest of our future reward? And, anyway, how did one set his affection on a vague concept of things above? How does one pour out of the deep emotional places of his heart a love for some vague, distant place? Obviously, he did not mean that.

The fifth verse begins to explain things above and things on the earth: "Therefore consider the members of your earthly body as dead to immorality, impurity, passion, evil desire, and greed, which amounts to idolatry" (Col. 3:5 NAS). These terms describe relationships to one another emanating from a deadly selfishness and a perverse greed. We were to turn our back on these things. Again, in verse 8, I noticed that we were to put aside, or "put off"—in Pauline language—"anger, wrath, malice, slander, and abusive speech from your mouth" (Col. 3:8 NAS). These were the things that are "on the earth." These are the things that have their source in the sinful, destructive nature and mind of man.

But how did one set his affection on "things above"? Where was "above" in Paul's mind? Verse 9 says simply: "Do not lie to one another, since you laid aside the old self with its evil practices, and have put on the new self who is being renewed to a true knowledge according to the image of the One who created him—a renewal in which there is no distinction between Greek and Jew, circumcised and uncircumcised, barbarian, Scythian, slave and freeman, *but Christ is all, and in all*" (Col. 3:9-11 NAS).

This is how you put on the mind of Christ; this is how you set your affections on things above! All of it is person-to-person relationships permeated by the love of Christ which is shed abroad in our hearts by the Holy Spirit. Again, it reflects John 15:10-12 that if we are to express our love to Jesus, in the way He prefers receiving it, we must simply pass on a similar love to others! What a marvelous coming together of the terrible dichotomy between secular and sacred. No wonder the Old Testament writer exclaimed with such joy: "The whole earth is full of His glory!"

When I love my brother I am indeed directly pouring love out to Jesus Christ! A second part of the ontological realism of Scripture and the promised theological presence of God became extremely clear. In His simple commandment to love one another Jesus had implicitly given us everything for which the human mind searches and the human heart longs. Jesus taught in John 14:21-23 that God would be totally and intimately and inwardly present to those who obeyed His commandment. This satisfies the search after God! Secondly, from Colossians 3, I learned that God receives His own satisfaction directly when we pour out our love to our fellow-man. When we love one another, we are directly loving Him!

Paul had suggested that we were to owe no man anything but to love one another for when we loved one another we fulfilled the law (Rom. 13:8). I suddenly saw that we would fulfill the *whole* law by so loving. Confirmation of this came to me from Galatians 5. In verse 1, Paul exhorts the Galatian Christians to stand fast in the freedom for which Christ had set them free and to not again become subject to the yoke of slavery which was the law that engenders sinful response. Paul said succinctly, "For in Christ Jesus neither circumcision nor uncircumcision means anything [sacramental emphases and differentiation are not as exciting to God as they are to ourselves], *but faith working through love*" (Gal. 5:6 NAS). James had suggested the same theme: "You see that faith was working with his works, and as a result of the works, faith was perfected" (James 2:22 NAS). John had said essentially the same thing: "And this is His commandment, that we believe in the name of His Son Jesus Christ, and love one another, just as He commanded us" (1 John 3:23 NAS). Notice again that faith is to be expressed toward Jesus Christ and love (faith's expression) is to be extended toward one another—the double commandment. Then Paul insures the simplicity of the message when he says, "For the whole Law is fulfilled in one word . . . *You shall love your neighbor as yourself*" (Gal. 5:14 NAS). *The whole Law* is fulfilled in the simple commandment of Jesus Christ to love one another, not just the last six commandments of the Decalogue.

Jesus has said simply in the Sermon on the Mount that we were to " 'Enter by the narrow gate; for the gate is wide, and the way is broad that leads to destruction, and many are those who enter by it. For the gate is small, and the way is narrow that leads to life, and few are those who find it' " (Matt. 7:13, 14 NAS). For so many years I had been taught simply that the way and the narrow gate was Jesus Christ. That is true, but I'd never noticed the context of this saying before: "Therefore, whatever you want others to do for you, do so for them, for *this is the Law and the Prophets!*" (Matt. 7:12 NAS). Here again the message concerns person-to-person relationships in love. To be sure, the gospel is not one of salvation by works, but of salvation through love which is imparted to us by the Holy Spirit. Nevertheless, this love is to be extended and expressed in a lavish manner to others. It is biblically incorrect and exegetically inaccurate to divorce verse 13 from verse 12. Such numerical divisions were not in the original.

Jesus, in this simple passage, is exposing His mind in a beautiful way. He, in brilliance, digests for us the utterly simple and beautiful meaning of the whole Old Testament in one single sentence. Nowhere is the mind of Jesus more explicitly seen than here.

Again, in Matthew 9:13 and 12:7, Jesus quotes Hosea 6:6 (see also Micah 6:6-8) and juxtaposes two qualities, one of which is highly desirable to God, and the other not desirable. If I was correct in seeing "sacrifice" as the costly offering of personal things to God and "mercy" as the expression of love and compassion to my fellow-man, then again the same message was explicitly stated by our Lord. Sacrifice is not desired by God. *He does not seek gifts from us for himself!* So much of our liturgical worship and offerings are not His desire. What He rather seeks for is an expression of love to the widow and the orphan and the distraught and the hurting and the lonely. How very perverted our religion has become. Traditionally, and all too frequently historically, we have emphasized "sacrifice" and have avoided "mercy." The latter is entirely delightful to God as the prophets make so utterly clear, and the former so utterly undesired. The sacrifice of God is a broken and contrite heart, one which recognizes the error of our relationships and destructive dealings with one another. That sacrifice is totally acceptable.

It began to make utter and complete sense. "And so, as those who have been chosen of God, holy and beloved, put on a heart of compassion, kindness, humility, gentleness and patience; bearing with one another, and forgiving each other, whoever has a complaint against any one; just as the Lord forgave you, so also should you. And beyond all these things put on love, which is the perfect bond of unity. And let the peace of Christ rule in your hearts, to which indeed you were called in one body; and be thankful" (Col. 3:12-15 NAS).

The way in which I set my affection on things above is by taking the explicit commandment of Jesus which embraces all of His other teachings and doing them by putting them into practice. In this way I assert my affectionate love for Him. In this way I set my affection on things above, things which have come to us from the living God. His Word is life. Obedience to His Word produces the divine life itself.

A parallel passage is found in 2 Peter: "For by these He has granted to us His precious and magnificent promises, in order that by them you might become partakers of the divine nature, having escaped the corruption that is in the world by lust. Now for this very reason also, applying all diligence, in your faith supply moral excellence [or as the KJV calls it, "virtue"], and in your moral excellence, knowledge; and in your knowledge, self-control, and in your self-control, perseverance, and in your perseverance, godliness; and in your godliness, brotherly kindness, and in your brotherly kindness, Christian love" (2 Pet. 1:4-7 NAS). Here again the emphasis is upon those qualities derived by the Holy Spirit and poured into our hearts to be reconstructed in us and through us to our fellow-man. This is the direction of all the Scriptures!

In Romans 1 the apostle Paul warns against the wrath of God, which is directed against ungodliness, the lack of reverence and faith in God which is accompanied by the consequent unrighteousness or destructive and sinful relationships toward each other. Paul then describes a decadent culture as one evidencing homosexuality. Following this, he breaks down sin into twenty-two component parts. A careful examination of these will reveal that each, with a possible single exception, describes person-to-person relationships shot through with the destructive power of selfishness and sin. The chapter concludes with the accompanying fracturing of human relationships, a polarization between persons and, finally, the hardening of the heart against one's fellow-man. In fact, the essence and end of sin is the destructive damming up of compassion in the human heart one for another. The existential root of sin evidenced in the joint sensuality and greed mentioned by Paul so often is the root of lovelessness for my fellow-man. The work of the Holy Spirit is to reintroduce the integrative and synthesizing power of love. Paul states this in many ways; perhaps the best example is: "That their hearts may be encouraged, having been knit together in love, and attaining to all the wealth that comes from the full assurance of understanding, resulting in a true knowledge of God's mystery, that is, Christ himself, in whom are hidden all the treasures of wisdom and knowledge" (Col. 2:2, 3 NAS).

When, in obedience to our Lord Jesus Christ, we truly display the love of Christ each to the other, with its purity, integrity, mercy, and compassion, we are in fact to enjoy the resident presence of the living God and His Son Jesus Christ powerfully in our inner beings. Likewise, when we love one another directly and with integrity of love, we are in fact directly expressing our love to Jesus Christ, for He resides in our brother as well as in ourselves. We are setting our affection on things above.

The Holy Spirit is the indwelling dynamic of Calvary love invading our being (Rom. 5:5). His is the work of introducing us into ever-increasing spheres of glory (2 Cor. 3:18). Paul had suggested in Galatians 5:22-23 that the horizontal thrust of love reproduced is the most perfect expression of the vertical love received from God.

Everywhere this message was confirmed to me. My reading from Genesis to Revelation and the book of Acts revealed an exciting demonstration of this in the early church. To be sure, the early Christians were not perfect, but no church is. But the depth of the brotherly love they felt for each other is clearly demonstrated in the book of Acts. The corresponding powerful administration of God in preaching with persuasive love is seen as a corollary of that love. "And with great power the apostles were giving witness to the resurrection of the Lord Jesus, and abundant grace was upon them all" (Acts 4:33 NAS).

Convinced in my mind and heart, I knew that my home needed this dimension of love and that the church I was serving certainly needed more of this love and less of my orthodox berating. John the Beloved had suggested that we love each other because He first loved us. What a romantic idea to love our wives as Christ has, in fact, already loved us. No more competition, no more combativeness but truly an attitude of serving each other. Love, according to the Word of God, is a *decision* more than it is an *emotion*. Also the kind of "rest" that is described in Hebrews 3 and 4 became actually attainable, because of "Faith which works by love." The peace promised in Colossians 3:15—in the context of the entire chapter—came to be expected as the fruit of this kind of relationship. The secret of authority, for which many search today, is found directly within the love commandment itself, an inner authority that is not, at the same time, authoritarian.

Such love as God's love for us retranslated into our human relationships certainly holds out immense hope for the very ecumenicity of the Holy Spirit, which all of us know deep within our hearts is the prayer and desire of God himself. Whereas sin is a destructive and disuniting force, the love shed abroad in our hearts by the Holy Spirit is a powerful, uniting dynamic.

Whereas I felt formerly that churches lacked this love, I began to see that insofar as their faith was legitimately placed in Jesus Christ, this love lay potentially in the hearts of all true believers. Too often theology had fragmented that which Christ came to unite. I sensed now that love was actually present in every believer's heart, but that it was dammed up by false expectations and wrong teaching. The churches didn't lack love; they simply had never been clearly taught.

I decided to employ the scientific method, to test this hypothesis through experimentation to see if it would lead to the actual, catalytic reactions I felt were contained within the hypothesis itself.

12

Husbands, So Love Your Wives

*To love anyone is nothing else than to wish that
person good.* (St. Thomas Aquinas)

Could it be that all God really wanted from me was for
me so to love Bette? It seemed utterly and ridiculously
simple and frankly not theological enough. Truth is
innately simple but was not this too simplistic? No
countering arguments appeared out of the text.
Everything I read seemed to suggest that God wanted
me to love my wife and my children in the same way and
to the same degree that He had loved me. Mentally
convinced that this was biblically solid, psychologically
promising, and delightful in every prospect, I said these
very words: "God, if that is what you want, that is what
you are going to get!" With that prayer, the decision was
made that I would begin the experiment at home. I
would endeavor, with God's support and the indwelling
Holy Spirit's inspiration, to love my wife as she had

never been loved before.

The very study of this message itself throughout the Bible had disclosed all too clearly the multiplied ways I had failed to grant to her the loving and affirming of life that every person needs. I had cheated her—not through infidelity—but by withholding from her the full joy of this kind of love. The bad humor and the cutting jokes and the self-preoccupations had cheated her of the very joys and promises of a husband-wife relationship. It was not too difficult to discern the innate selfishness of a great deal of my behavior, and I recognized how giving and loving my dear wife had been.

She knew that I loved her. That was obvious even in spite of many shortcomings. Yet we both sensed within our marriage a failure to achieve that kind of free communication and open, avowed love that can make a marriage so beautiful.

Defining "spirituality" as I had previously done, made her appear to me not very "spiritual." She certainly did not spend enough time in the Bible! She was not notorious for attending prayer meetings. She seemed to avoid that kind of spiritual dialogue that my heart yearned for. She seemed put off by the spiritual jargon of so many who claimed to be in the "inner circle." Frankly, there were many times that I felt she was not reaching those spiritual heights that were available if one pressed on. Furthermore, she seemed to have no desire to do so. This really aggravated me.

Frequently and unfortunately I would express this to her. "Why don't you read the Bible more?" She also seemed altogether too natural and too cheerful to be truly Christian! She loved gardening and flowers and laughter and good times. All of these things added up in my mind at that time to the conclusion that she was not going on with Christ as she ought. Whereas the general atmosphere of our life together was one of caring, it was clouded over by these mutually contradictory expectations.

To begin with, Bette had not really wanted to be a minister's wife. In fact, when we were engaged to be married she wanted me to go into business, because certain friends of hers had predicted she would end up marrying a clergyman. This she avowed she would never do. While I was to later discover that her love for Jesus was in fact very real and very deep, it did not take the forms I thought it should.

Constantly I had pressured her to change, and to become the perfect minister's wife. Now part of my vow was to just love her, accept her, and enjoy her!

I remembered Immanuel Kant's marvelous dictum: "Never use another person as a means to your ends but always as ends in themselves." What did I have to lose? A stuffy and unenjoyable Christianity? Better to lose it than to hold on to it. Lose traditions? They had never served me that well. Anyway the prospect of loving Bette in this marvelous way seemed altogether too delicious not to try it.

Secretly and without divulging it to my dear wife, I made a resolve before God that this in fact was the way I was going to proceed. Wouldn't she be surprised? I savored this possibility. I remembered sometime in my past when upon coming home she had said to me quietly but with sincere desperation, "Len, I love you very much, but get off my back!" That was it—I was pressing too hard to achieve certain goals and to change certain facets of her personality. I could see now how utterly ugly that was in the light of Paul's and my Lord's recommendations. What terrible pressures I had placed her under. But that would change. And change it did.

Jesus had promised that if we would give, it should be given back to us in full measure, "pressed down, and shaken together, and running over, shall men give" into our hands (Luke 6:38). This was no less true in our home. Love, says Paul, edifies; that is it builds the other person up. It releases the other person to be himself and contributes to his growth and maturation by freeing him from the manipulation of another. Love enjoys the actual human being we confront. Love is very human, though divinely imparted.

Bette was stunned the first time I preached this message: "To love one another as Christ loved us." Later in the car she said: *"That's it; that's what it's all about!"* She later shared with me that all of her life as a confessing Christian she had tried to walk as she had been taught in an evangelical church background, but she was never satisfied.

Neither one of us realized in those early days the dramatic discoveries and changes we would make together as we explored the ramifications of this message. A true discovery it was. As we began to develop this message and share it in our home our communication with each other deepened. From the most tender moments and the most intimate to the most joyous laughter between the two of us, we began to rediscover what God intended marriage to be like. Jesus had promised our joy would be full and literally it overflowed from our beings.

At times I was troubled that I was not pious enough. I did not know whether I was backsliding into her point of view or she was in fact joining me in a third dimension of Christian reality. We discovered that the competition and antagonisms between male and female are truly over when love reigns in our hearts. This is as Paul promises: "There is neither . . . male nor female. . ." (Gal. 3:28).

One morning while seated at the kitchen table, I said to her: "Honey, I have learned more from you this past year than I have learned all my life at the university and seminary and I am truly grateful." I could never have admitted this before. Disturbed by the tears that came into her eyes, I inquired if I had offended her.

"Quite the contrary," she assured me, and she went on to explain that she had never expected me to say something that humble. In previous years she had told me that I would probably read every book that was written while life itself would pass me by. Christ's love supplied a new dimension of listening to each other and it built bridges of communication between us.

Our home became the laboratory where this love between us flourished. Both Bruce, our son, and Carole, our daughter, warmed in a beautiful and unfolding way to this love between their mother and dad. This love proved during their teen years to be the finest incubation of Christianity for them. A familiar plaque in our home says it simply: "The greatest gift a father can give to his children is to love their mother." We never had a single day's problem with either. Moreover, they seemed to love being at home. They did not seek to find fulfillment outside but their friends came to our house. Many of their friends and ours would exclaim after short periods in our home that they had never felt so peaceful or so close to God. Many began to inquire as to what this secret was and we happily shared it with them.

Paul meant just what he said when he wrote: "Husbands, love your wives, even as Christ also loved the church, and gave himself for it; That he might sanctify and cleanse it with the washing of water by the word, That he might present it to himself a glorious church, not having spot, or wrinkle, or any such thing" (Eph. 5:25-27). Humorously, I often think a man ultimately gets the wife he deserves. Either he contributes to her great beauty and winsomeness of character or by his failure so to love, he creates the nagging and critical woman with whom it is frequently so hard to live. Thank God for my Betts!

13

Misunderstanding

*Love is the hardest lesson in Christianity; but, for
that reason, it should be most our care to learn it.*
(William Penn)

We felt we had stumbled on "the pearl of great price."
Naturally, we wanted to share it with those people who
meant the most to us. As we elatedly discovered
Scripture after Scripture defining human relationships in
Christ, we could scarcely contain the desire to share
them with our congregation.

For total fulfillment, a man needs to find satisfaction
not only in his home but also, and quite especially, in his
vocation. Sensing completion in one very basic human
relationship, we desired to see if it were transferable to a
larger body and a corporate experience. We just knew
that the congregation would be as excited and elated as
we were becoming.

To our utter amazement, the people seemed to lack
any perception of what we were saying or to display any

response. They sought for "deeper" spiritual teaching.

One can understand how divorce takes place in the secular world between two fine people who suddenly discover they're moving in two different directions. The pain and trauma is in no way lessened by the fact that neither party wishes it. There is an affection between them that nonetheless seems incapable of bridging the differences in their goals and expectations. Some were pleading for a supernaturalism which would become convincing to those outside and cause the fire to fall from off the altar. They desired to be "closer to God." I was discovering a way to do this by coming closer to my fellow Christian, my fellow-man.

Loving them as we did and knowing that they cared as much for us as we did for them, I felt a sense of pain and trauma. I was beginning to sense the love commandment of Jesus as the ultimate secret of the universe and key to all things promised by God. They saw holiness to be the ultimate, interpreted as a personal vertical relationship to God. They knew, as I did, that it all began in the love of God for man, received by faith. In this we were both in agreement. But many in the congregation seemed to feel the natural love which might flow from this to the other person needed purification by offering that love first to God in some strange way and then to man. They saw love for each other as an "inevitable consequence" flowing out of great "inwardness." The main thrust was thus always inward and constant. They sensed, it seemed to me, that that great love would someday come when our inward relationship to God was made complete by some supernatural thrust of God himself in response to intense prayer and intense inwardness.

There was a love for each other but not the dangerous, universal love of John 3:16. The love they were willing to show involved the propagation of a message. In that regard, they loved deeply. It seemed that people were only objects for evangelism or spiritual aggression.

We often proselytize and traditionalize and conceptualize until the adventure of love is destroyed. G.K. Chesterton wrote, "The Christian ideal has not been tried and found wanting; it has been found difficult and left untried."

As I struggled within the context of this experience to share with my charismatic brethren the love of Christ as I was seeing it, some old questions surfaced: What would a church be like that took with utmost seriousness and simplicity the love commandment to be its key and its guide? Why do Christians who obviously love the Lord Jesus fail to take this as centrally as Christ commanded it? Why do we fail to interpret the love of the cross—and the cross Christ invited us to carry—as dying for our enemies? Could we follow the Christ who so endangers our securities?

The more we wanted to share the visions and insights we loved, the more we sadly sensed we were growing apart from these good people. We were not listening to the same trumpet call that they were.

14

Transition

God's love is not a conditional love; it is an open-hearted, generous self-giving which God offers to men. Those who would carefully limit the operation of God's love . . . have missed the point. (J.B. Phillips)

Someone recently suggested in our pulpit that Jesus did not practice what He preached but rather preached what He practiced! Humorously, I often envisaged myself approaching St. Peter's Gate with sheaths of sermons in my hands containing introductions, three major points, subheadings, and major conclusions. Inwardly, I questioned whether we should seek some practical outlet for this love beyond the local church and its meetings. Would not God also demand that we care for those in prisons, for those who are naked, for those who are deeply hurt by life? If He sought some great active service of love from us, we would seek to be alert to His call. Was it enough simply to accept the role of a teacher and to transmit this message to the largest number of persons?

During this time of searching for my own expression of this in the church and through the church to the outside world and questioning my role as a teacher to which I believed God had called me, we waited for an indication of His mind.

A call arrived from Dr. Victor Dawe, pastor of the Neshannock Presbyterian Church in New Wilmington, Pennsylvania, to conduct a week of spiritual emphasis there. New Wilmington is a lovely college town situated approximately twenty miles across the border from Youngstown, Ohio. How pleased I was by the large numbers of men who came to the breakfasts, the ladies who poured in for the late morning messages and the crowded church at night. An immense excitement hovered over the congregation.

Throughout the week we developed the search of our hearts and the love commandment and its implications. The response was magnificent. Night after night persons committed their lives in a new way to Jesus Christ and seemed to catch this message.

I will never forget the closing Friday night service. I preached the concluding message with a sense of excitement. As a preacher, I generally observe the audience very carefully. At times, I single out people for personal and deep observation to note their reactions and to insure that I am "locking in" with the audience. That evening, out of hundreds present, one man, Mr. Bill Bair, a close friend of Pastor Dawe and a lay pastor in a Methodist church, completely absorbed my attention. I happened to notice that Bill was writing furiously as I spoke. This was nice, because I thought he was taking down notes of what I said. But when I saw that he did not cease writing when I paused, it became apparent that he was not really listening at all. That intrigued and slightly irritated me. It was my particular notice of this that God was to use in Bill's life in a beautiful way.

Deep within, Bill was searching for his own obedience to the love commandment. All his life he had dreamed of working with children in trouble with the law. He had a longing to serve their needs. During the week, unknown to anyone else, God was giving him a concept of a foundation that could work with court-awarded teenagers. Just a few years away from possible retirement he was beginning to feel that possibly God was calling him to this kind of work immediately. So he decided to put out a fleece. "God, if it is you speaking to me, have our guest preacher, this evening, while preaching, mention my name from the pulpit!"

Imagine Mr. Bair's complete surprise, when in the next five minutes, I addressed three rhetorical questions to him directly from the pulpit: "Isn't that right, Mr. Bair?" Three times, and not just once. I had never done that before. Moreover, it was remarkable that I remembered his name for apart from several encounters that week we hardly knew anybody there. I was extremely fascinated with his preoccupation, which led to the eruption of those three questions. Alone and knowing of that inner fleece he had put out to God in the silence of his heart, he was startled by hearing his wife say to him, "Bill, aren't you going to answer Mr. Evans?" Gesturing a startled response to the pulpit, he relapsed into an inward and awesome conversation with his heart and with God.

Bill has told this beautiful story in his own autobiography, *Love Is an Open Door.* Suffice it to say that before the night was over he walked to the pulpit just after the benediction, and shared with the congregation what had taken place in his heart and in his mind and assured them he was obeying the call of God to leave his work as a lay pastor, a part-time builder, and as a public relations salesman for the gas company in order to initiate the Bair Foundation and the work to which he now knew God was calling him. He then asked the congregation, or those members of it who felt this was of God, to join him at the altar where he would descend the chancel steps, and ask Mr. Evans to consecrate him.

If Bill Bair was startled at the response of God to his inner fleece, I was equally startled by one of the most amazing responses I had seen in my years as a preacher. Here was a man who heard the message for one week, and was willing to commit his whole life to it. Could it be an answer to the question I was asking in my heart: "Is it enough for me to teach?" Not that I would not love those I taught and related to, not that I would not seek to express love to all that I came across, but would it be sufficient for me just to emphasize this message so that others could catch it? Was God indicating that if I faithfully preached it, He would in turn cause those works to be initiated which would increasingly perform and do the very acts of love I was teaching?

Today, after ten years, we have seen the Bair Foundation grow from its small beginnings to a beautiful work where, during this year alone, one hundred young people will be ministered to. In addition, out of the ministry of Bill Bair and his associates, multiplied hundreds—if not thousands—have come to Christ.

It is enough for a man to follow his own call in the economy of God. God will weave ministries together which will express His total will and purpose. None of us is by himself the total ministry, but rather each of us, affecting other lives, will cause that totality of service and love to be ministered to the world in Jesus' name.

15

A New Opportunity

All loves should be simply stepping-stones to the love of God. So it was with me; and blessed be his name for his great goodness and mercy. (Plato)

Pleasant Valley Evangelical Church of Niles, Ohio, is located approximately twenty miles from the Bair Foundation in New Wilmington, Pennsylvania. A small, independent church, they had been looking for three years for a pastor. A number of persons from Ohio had been present in those meetings in the Neshannock Presbyterian Church and carried the news of a pastor they were excited about to the pulpit committee. The chairman of the committee obtained a series of tapes of my messages and listened to them carefully for several months before proposing my name to the pulpit committee. The nominating committee then listened to the same tapes and finally presented them to the larger congregation. Now that our tapes had been heard by more than just the pulpit committee, the question of the charismatic experience had at least quietly been shared among the members, since there was a prospect I might be called to their church as a pastor if the congregation so desired. The membership was comprised of a small group of people who had been together, many of them across the years, and there were strong family interrelationships. It would be fair to say that a strong anti-ecumenical emphasis had likewise been fostered in their midst. Eventually, the pulpit committee recommended us to the church and we came to candidate.

I will never forget the day I went there to preach in the morning and evening services. Naturally, having the dream of a church that would be both strongly evangelistic and thoroughly loving, I shared my search and discovery of the theology of the love commandment. In the evening, as I developed the theology underlying the love commandment, I did so almost passionately, praying that they would capture my dream. At the end of the message, I issued a call to the church (prior to their call to us!) that if they desired me to come as their pastor, they would come forward and consecrate themselves to walk together with me in that mutuality of love and close harmony and desire to express love to the world outside. I must have been powerfully persuasive, for only a few came forward.

Sadly within my heart I knew even prior to closing the service, that I would not accept a call to that church because I sensed I would be a difficulty to them if they did not understand. Just at that time, however, a small and very thin lady, whom I assumed to be a member of the congregation, rose from her seat and proceeded down the center aisle toward the pulpit. I wondered why she was coming, and asked her if she wanted to say something. She quietly said, "No." Still she proceeded to come to the pulpit.

Astonished by this reaction to my sermon, I asked a second question, "Why are you coming?"

She replied, "I am a Roman Catholic, and I have waited seventeen years to hear this message. I want to stand with you in your closing prayer." And she did.

We stood with our arms around each other, as I quietly led the congregation in prayer, with tears streaming down my cheeks. To me it was a sign from God that He was calling me to this pulpit and I could accept the call, and that He would be with me. Incidentally, many people seemed quietly, after that incident, to come forward for prayer. How I unceasingly thank God for the remarkable action of that lovely Catholic sister.

The call was extended and we accepted and looked forward to serving this church.

Then I experienced my first heart attack in April of 1969. During the time of convalescence I again felt the deep measure of love that a husband and a wife can know of caring in a real situation of interpersonal need. Additionally, innumerable messages of concern and love reached us from all across the country.

I began to wonder what the church we were going to serve felt about having "half a man" as a preacher, one whose heart had already given an indication of physical need. I would certainly not have the robust vitality of former years. Would they feel locked in? Certainly, they gave no such indication. Finally, after a creative period of rethinking the meaning of life, I began ministering in our present parish on July 1, 1969.

Naturally, I began to preach the simple message of Jesus: that we were to love one another as God first loved us. Compelled by this dream, I admit that perhaps I was somewhat one-sided in my proclamation. Some were made extremely cautious and anxious by the implied "ecumenicity" of the love commandment. Some felt we should just preach the simple gospel of God's love for men and leave the result of the walk to the Holy Spirit.

From time to time the pulpit committee met with me and suggested, in a very gracious way, that they indeed liked the message, but couldn't we preach something else as well? While it was true, they insisted, that love was central, there were many other things of equal importance that could be preached. It was not so much that I could not consent to that, but I knew that the greatest need in the churches was the manifestation of this love to the world.

Gradually, individuals began to be drawn to the emphasis of Jesus Christ to love one another as He had loved us. There were other people who felt threatened by this consistent emphasis as detracting from the gospel itself.

The congregation was extremely cautious and guarded, and some were even openly questioning. Having been taught that the ecumenical church might be the dangerous entity described by the book of the Revelation, and that the Roman Catholic institution might be its eventual recrudescence, they were naturally apprehensive at the pastor's open avowals of love for Roman Catholic people. The strong prayers of their new pastor, that God would put His arms of love about the bishop, and put His arms of love around the Roman Catholic parishes, and pour out His lovely Holy Spirit upon them, must have astonished them in the light of their earlier teaching. New ideas take time to grow.

No matter where I started to preach, the love message eventually came through. Some felt the message was too concessionary, others too ecumenical, others too liberal, others too humanistic. In spite of these misgivings, it soon became apparent that numbers of new people began to seek out the little church on the back country road. Rather astonishingly they seemed to respond to the love of God preached in this indirect way and were turning over their lives to Him. At first it was not a great rush of people, but it was noted that they came from various backgrounds.

The truth about Jesus Christ is very specific and unchanging. The good news of the gospel is a reality revealed by God through His Spirit. The love of God is universal and intended for every man. God's love is infinite and given to the whole world to be received by faith. The measure of that love is limitless. The reality and power of that love is exposed in the cross of Christ and His resurrection.

The New Testament writer, James, portrays this love not only as being merciful but also *impartial* (without respect of persons!) (James 2:1-26). Paul describes this love as intended not only to be given to our brother in Christ but, by its very nature and extension, to all mankind (1 Thess. 3:12-13). James insists that this love is a total, complete attitude: "Does a fountain send out from the same opening both fresh and bitter water?" (James 3:11 NAS). The love of God, this royal law, is infinite, unlimited, universally extended, impartial, explosive, and magnetic.

Could a church having been touched by His love take the love commandment as its operating principle and goal? Would a corporate body of believers risk that challenge and dare to leave the shoals of dogmatic security for the dangerous depths of such love for each other and their fellow-men? I wondered, prayed, dreamed, and at times feared. To be sure, individuals like Mother Teresa of Calcutta dared so to love. Intuitively I knew the magnetic healing power of such a love, the joyous freedom, and living, perceptual excitement.

Our people were deeply evangelistic, committed to true holiness of life and character. Along with this came a fear of dissipating the pure gospel with imbalanced social gospel emphases, the almost bald humanism of much preaching, and the absence of strong evangelism. They had finally freed themselves from denominational ties when they felt these would tend to obscure the good news. Moreover, they had been indoctrinated to fear the coming "world church" and a dangerous "ecumenism" which would water down the gospel. They were totally committed to a bold, clear evangel and wary of anything less than this.

They had paid a price for this stand. When their small denomination merged with a larger one over a decade ago, they had decided to go it alone to ensure freedom to preach the Word of God. They lost their beloved small church building and a substantial amount of money to the merger. For three years as a small, independent church, they had prayerfully searched for a pastor who would not only lovingly lead them but would share their fervor for the gospel of Jesus Christ, for missions, and for their major concerns.

Then we came affirming these same goals, but with a dream of a loving and unified church and a message which sounded dangerously close to humanism with an "ecumenicalism" of the Holy Spirit, an "ecumenicalism" of love.

One cannot receive Jesus' love commandment into his heart seriously and remain as he was or where he was. To receive Christ's powerful and universal and personal love is shattering to all man-made boundaries, dangerous to prejudice, threatening to traditions, and destructive to arrogance and fear.

I had sensed for years—as I studied the love commandment and all the related passages I could find throughout Scripture—the frightening dimensions and extensions of this love. The congregation, likewise, as they heard this reiterated preaching on love, began to sense the same frightening and unknown dimensions of love. Where would love lead them? What strange bedfellows would result? What essential truths might be lost, altered, or dissipated?

I well understood their fears for most of them had also been mine as I was led along year after year in the further exploration of the love message.

As shattering as Peter's encounter with Cornelius was, it could hardly be greater than the shattering caused by the outpouring of the Holy Spirit upon the lovely Roman Catholics in 1966 and subsequent years. It brought the earth-shaking awareness to countless minds that God's love was not a ghetto love. Our boundaries and sacred traditions were not necessarily His! Our vaunted orthodoxies sacredly insuring our separations were scorched by the hot wind of His love. We would be forced by God himself to reexamine our man-made boundaries and terrible lovelessness which we masked in many ways.

As the new pastor and the congregation came together it is needless to say there was misunderstanding, trauma, and anxiety. Did we use the same words but mean opposingly different things? Need the pastor constantly exhort the saints to "love one another"? No matter where the sermon began it seemed to end there. With dry humor some quipped that even if I preached on the "Three Young Men in the Fiery Furnace" it could come out "Love One Another!"

Some even suggested if I didn't change the message they would have to pray us out of the pulpit. There was obvious dismay in the ranks.

Others, more diplomatically, admitted the truth behind the message, even the importance of it, and then suggested a more balanced approach. It was like telling Oral Roberts to balance his "seed faith" preaching. This message was not mine by dilettante choice or option. It resulted from painstaking growth and search and discovery—dare we hallow it and say "revelation"? Certainly no prophet or apostle ever felt a greater compulsion to share his message than I did.

And share it I did from the pulpit, privately in homes, in the office, in seminars, conferences, and wherever I was given the opportunity. Multiplied thousands of tapes went out each year not only through our local church but in conferences as well. I confess that my delivery was impassioned, my excitement was genuine. I sought to share that which "turned me on." Many times I would invite young men and young women or groups of young men and young women or any others who were interested to my office. I would invite them to come and bring a tape recorder and numbers of tapes so that they could record my long and arduous search on their recorders, and share the multiplied Scriptures which had come alive for me. Then they could study in their leisure the things they were learning hurriedly in my office. I felt the tape would preserve the content and they could hear it over and over again.

Gradually, though numbers of people remained uptight by the accent of the pulpit, some relaxed and felt comfortable with me personally and even comfortable with (or inured to!) the message. After all it was not extra-biblical! Jesus did *command* it! Then again it might even be a good suggestion!

During those early years a young people's revolution took place. Many youth were turning to Jesus Christ in the cities of Youngstown and Warren and surrounding communities. Their enthusiasm for Jesus was real and sincere. A large percentage of these young people found their way to our fellowship. Soon we had hundreds of college and high school students crowding in. In spite of their new ways and at times strange dress and unorthodox music, they were warmly and lovingly received. Perhaps the preaching had been a preparation, after all. The people did not see their strange dress, they were not then turned off by their strange music, but rather were able to look into their faces and see human beings whom God profoundly loved and whom they had been invited to receive and love in Christ's name. As a result, the young people went out into the streets and enthusiastically shared with other youth that they had found a church where they would be accepted and loved exactly as they were. The young people even came to us and asked for cards with maps showing the location of the church, so they could invite others to come. They would sing with their guitars, and they brought a hand-clapping style to our evening meetings. To be sure this did not represent the musical style of the local church and, I must confess, not necessarily my own background of classical music, but we recognized the work of God in their lives.

The services grew in attendance from about 100 in the morning and 60 in the evening to where our small sanctuary, seating about 250, was completely full. Moreover, as this love was given and received, increasing numbers were being drawn excitingly to a saving knowledge of Jesus Christ as their Savior and Lord. This strange, new message was in fact causing people to come to Christ in ways that were unprecedented in the past history of the church. It seemed to have its own power to draw people to God. Undeniably more and more stories surfaced from persons whose lives were transformed, people who were coming to Christ for salvation, others who were being healed in their bodies and many who were being filled with the Holy Spirit. Divorced people were being reunited, marriages were being transformed, and family relationships were changed. Unsolicited testimonies began to accumulate of the marvelous experiences people were having because of coming to our meetings.

The love we shared heightened our sense of joy. And this in turn began to draw further numbers of people in to see what was happening. Bette and I had been experiencing this in our marriage, but now people were feeling the same joy and the same excitement resulting from the mutual love of Christ and love for each other in the corporate body of the church.

This joy and love caused the little church to grow from a total of several hundred in the two services to between fourteen hundred and two thousand. As I write this now in October of 1977, last Sunday we had just about three thousand at our two services as Larry Tomczak, a long-time friend of our congregation, preached for us.

When Larry summoned those who had never committed themselves to Jesus Christ as their Lord and Savior, some three hundred stood and publicly declared they were coming to Christ. Each Sunday, for five years without fail, multiplied numbers have not only come to Jesus Christ but subsequently demonstrated His love and shared strong witness. One lovely lady, in the thirteen months after she had committed her life to Christ, brought twenty-three members of her family to the Lord by the radiance of her life and the quiet power of her witness. She led six co-workers to Jesus at the office! Another man, planning to kill several persons in the subsequent week, came one night in 1976, gave his life to Jesus Christ and in three months led twelve of his family to the Lord!

Church became exciting. Many were drawn there by word of mouth from a large radius. When asked why they came, they characteristically responded: "You can *feel* the love!" "You *feel* relaxed, accepted!" "You *feel* God's presence!" None has said it was the power of our preaching! Most, however, do confess that the preaching has changed their lives and the message has revolutionized their Christian life styles.

Church became thrilling and exciting and beautiful for me as well. To see the love in faces erupting into joy and laughter at times, reaching out to and from the pulpit so that my very heart leaped with joy, caused me and others to rush to church early. This was also partly out of necessity. We had enlarged our little sanctuary at that time to comfortably seat approximately three hundred forty people. We remembered the first Sunday after we enlarged it. The sanctuary was completely full. It seemed that every time we expanded there were people there to fill it. Eventually we often had to cram seven hundred to nine hundred people into the little church, all the while praying that the fire department would be compassionate toward us. Once when Larry Tomczak preached in the small sanctuary the crowd stood outside in drizzling rain looking in through the open windows to capture some of the excitement and joy. I later learned the ushers passed the offering plate out on the lawn! One person left his seat to go to the washroom, while another climbed in the window and took it!

The enlarged sanctuary, dedicated in January, 1976, to seat nine hundred sixty people was soon filled to capacity. Probably one-third of our evening congregation consists of practicing Roman Catholics. We gratefully thank God for the work of His Holy Spirit in bringing us love and unity we had never dreamed of before.

Owen Owens, a loved lay leader who had formerly held negative feelings toward Roman Catholics, loves to tell how he accompanied me and others to a Roman Catholic school in Cleveland where I was to give a witness on Sunday afternoon to several hundred Catholic charismatics. He and some others loved me enough to go but kept tentative and cautious guards up. This was in those "early days." During a coffee break, "Big O," as we call Owen, went for coffee and a donut. He stands about six feet three inches tall. A very short nun walked up to talk to him. Looking up with a lovely expression on her face, she asked this strong evangelical from a Pentecostal background: "Sir, do you know my Jesus as I do?" Stunned and discomfited, he blurted out: "I go to Pleasant Valley!" Quietly and lovingly, she replied: "Yes, but do you know and love Jesus as your Savior and Lord as I do?" She was stressing an essential truth he well knew: that it is not church membership that saves but a personal relationship with the living Lord Jesus Christ. His reeducation had begun.

As our people were exposed in love to the quiet witness of others, their lovely, open hearts recognized the broad love of Jesus Christ and the persuasive operation of God by His Holy Spirit in all! This is not to say there were not problems or that all changed rapidly. But as we all struggled together to seek God's will, admitted mistakes of zeal (mostly mine), the Holy Spirit continued to lead and guide.

Then I prayed that God would send thirty young people to study for the ministry in the next five years. In less than three years, some sixty young people left to various training centers and seminaries feeling a call of God upon their lives. Many lovely and wonderful stories proliferate, ministries develop, but this single fact of the youth excitedly following the call of God has thrilled my heart. They have seen, experienced, and thrilled to the saving grace and love of God as we have. They have known the joy of fellowship in that love, and feel the wonder of it all keenly with us.

16

Accept One Another

*The heart of him who truly loves is a paradise on
earth; he has God in himself, for God is love.*
(Abbé Félicité Robert de Lamennais)

Frequently, I have expanded and defined "wisdom"
as "the God-given art of creative, exciting, adventurous,
fulfilling, experimental, just, honest, loving,
compassionate, humble, forgiving, accepting, gentle,
kind, and warm human relationships."

That our world desperately needs this kind of wisdom
is all too clearly seen. The rise of feelings of alienation is
seen in newspaper reporting of man's failure to cope
with his fellow-man at home and abroad. Mounting
crime, divorce, the drug culture, racial tensions,
violence, and fear reflect man's inability to love
adequately.

The pastor's counseling office reveals as well the
traumatic family breakups occurring within the church.
The counseling load of human problems is

overwhelming. Our failure to cope successfully with others—even in marriage and home relationships—is apparent to all. The polarizing forces in human experience are powerful among nations, leading to "wars and rumors of wars." The same polarizing tendencies can be seen among churches where polarization takes place within the local church or between professing Christians of differing denominations. Pastors often fear and avoid other pastors, churches repudiate other churches, theologies compete with other theologies, dogmas are elevated to absolutes and persons are categorized, classified, pigeonholed, theologized—everything takes place *except* acceptance and love as Christ accepts and loves. We have tried everything else but simple obedience to Jesus' commandment to love one another as He has loved us. Consequently, we have reaped war and divorce (separation)—the two signs of our failure to cope, the marks of the lack of God's wisdom in our hearts.

But God has invited us to ask Him for wisdom (James 1:5) and defined it as "first pure, then peaceable, gentle, and easy to be intreated, full of mercy and good fruits, without partiality, and without hypocrisy" (James 3:13-17). Paul has put love through a prism in 1 Corinthians 13 and broken it down into its beautiful and humble parts and called it "the better way." Peter has analyzed the ultimate love—Calvary love, atoning love—by seeing Christ's death as "the just for the unjust that he might bring us to God!" (1 Pet. 3:18; also study 1 Pet. 2:11-4:1). This atoning love was not exhausted at

Calvary but it was set free in the energy of His Spirit to our generation through us. James calls it "the royal law" and John, in his epistles, makes "love" the *very* opposite of sin and transgression.

"Pastor Evans, you *radicalize* the message!" Yes, I do and have because in all my years and church life it was submerged and blended and lost in religious terminology. We have circumscribed it, qualified it, domesticated it, hidden it, and failed to practice and believe it.

If Jesus Christ be truly, and in fact, the Son of God and gives us one commandment, if truly He is our wisdom, then does it not make sense that this single commandment is the key to all life, the foundation of all realized dreams and aspirations of faith (Gal. 5:6, 14) and the source of the abundant life?

For pastors and church leaders the simple cry is to believe, experiment, and try. Or as the New Testament says, "taste and see." The believer or the church is designated by Jesus as "The salt of the earth . . . the light of the world" (Matt. 5:13, 14). How my own heart leaped as a beloved physician friend of mine, touched by this message, said to me simply one day: "Salt equals love!" He saw this to be true from the statement of Jesus. The moment he said it my own heart consented fully. "And if the salt has lost its saltness, wherewith shall it be salted?" If we have lost our love, our first love which is that dynamic love with which we respond to God and which issues in a prolific love for our fellow-man, where again shall we find it?

Perhaps the clearest statement of this love principle is

found in 1 John 4:7-12! God *is* love and He exhibits and defines this love in His action towards us. Then He clearly pleads for love (1 John 4:8) and states the logic of love's response to such love given: "Beloved, if God so loved us, *we ought also to love one another*" (1 John 4:11). He had earlier declared this pervasive New Testament logic: "Hereby perceive we the love of God, because he laid down his life for us: and *we ought to lay down our lives for the brethren*" (1 John 3:16).

The Word of God clearly defines what will take place as a result of this action. God will dwell in us and His love will become perfected in us (1 John 4:12). "My Father will love you, and I will love you and I will manifest myself to you!" Could anything be clearer? This message constantly recurs from Genesis to Revelation.

Sometime ago, a friend in southern Ohio, a fine businessman, requested a list of Scriptures that would support this general commandment of Jesus. He wanted to study the subject in depth. Hurriedly, I drew up the "Love List" and sent it to him. Since then, it has gone across the world, and has been carefully studied by thousands and has inspired many to take up the adventure of love. I hope you will be inspired to undertake this same adventure with us.

At one time on the mission field three thousand persons sat down simultaneously to study these passages in various parts of a particular South American country. This list of Scriptures can be found at the back of this book for you to study at leisure for your own inspiration. Frequently, when I speak I humorously repeat to the audience that God has said to all of us through His Son: "Try it, you'll like it!"

And they are trying it. Churches around the world and here at home, prison fellowships, families, pastors, boards, husbands and wives—these all have tried it and report it is true and works exactly as prescribed.

A small church in Ohio heard the message, believed, and committed themselves to love both in expression and action. They exploded spiritually and grew numerically so fast that they have a problem: how to provide adequate facilities for unbelievable growth and expansion.

In January of 1977 we visited New Zealand. There I shared the "love message" with a small Presbyterian congregation near Wellington. In September of the same year, I received a phone call from a traveling businessman from that congregation in New Zealand. He happened to be in Dayton on business, and through his call he revealed that their hoped-for growth and spiritual renewal took place within six months after they responded to the message. Previously, they had planned for such renewal to take years, but through love they had reached a point where they were forced to build and to expand their staff. Lovingly, he thanked me for having come to be with them. He stated simply that all of them in the church believed it was their reception of that message that inspired such tremendous growth.

Recently, I received a letter from a Baptist pastor in a large city in Alaska. He shared how tapes had reached him—a series upon the love commandment—through his deacons at a time of spiritual need and even difficulty within the church. They heard the message, listened, and believed together and the turn around was so swift and unbelievable and the result so beautiful that they wanted me to fly up at any time I chose to share their joy.

Finally, a man called from the Sacramento Valley of California several years ago to say he had heard this message when I was in Anaheim, California. At that time he simply thought it was "nice" and promptly dismissed it from his mind.

The next year, he informed us, he returned to the same conference where thousands were gathered to hear various teachers of the Word. Remembering our "nice talk" on love, he determined not to hear it again.

All the speakers at the conference had been assigned different rooms for their teaching sessions. I was assigned to a large auditorium. He continued by saying he preferred to hear another teacher who was ministering in a small room, but it was so crowded he could not get in. Reluctantly and resignedly, he returned to the auditorium where I was preaching. I appreciated his honesty.

Then quietly he began to share with me how he "began to hear, perceive, and believe. And then I got tremendously excited!" he exclaimed.

Suddenly, he realized it was not only a "nice" message, but was actually a "lost" message. He shared how he came to each subsequent teaching session early, with his Bible and note paper and tape recorders ready.

With deep love he went on to express his fervent affection for me and his sincere gratitude for the teaching. To my joy, he then said he was reproducing those tapes as fast as he could and had distributed them widely and broadly throughout the whole Sacramento Valley to all the pastors he knew within that region and hundreds of lay people as well. He continued on to assure me he knew of at least ten churches which were experiencing a direct, revolutionary renewal and expansion as a result of the pastors and the laymen believing that message in their hearts and experiencing it between themselves by decision and choice. Only then did he indicate that he too was a pastor.

"Why do you call me 'Lord, Lord,' and do not do what I say?" (Luke 6:46 NAS). The Lord's logic must become our logic if we are to see our homes and churches restored and renewed to the pristine affection and love which incubates a powerful proclamation of God's love. The Bible declares Jesus to be "the wisdom of God"! If He has given *one* commandment, is it not then logical that this commandment contains the secret of the universe, the sufficient rule for renewal of our hearts and our lives and our fellowships? His commandment becomes at the same time His invitation for all of us to experiment in the simplicity of adventurous obedience to *love, love, love.*

Love List

A new commandment I give unto you, That ye love one another; as I have loved you, that ye also love one another. By this shall all men know that ye are my disciples, if ye have love one to another. (John 13:34, 35)

NEW TESTAMENT PASSAGES.

A. Matthew.

1. Matt. 5-7 (Notice how much of the Sermon on the Mount is devoted to person-to-person love).
2. Matt. 9:13 and 12:7 (Mercy rather than sacrifice).
3. Matt. 15:1-20.
4. Matt. 18:1-35 (Compare verses 23-35 with James 2:12, 13).
5. Matt. 22:34-40 (Compare with Matt. 7:12-29).
6. Matt. 25:1-13 (Parable of the Wise and Foolish Virgins; compare with Luke 12:13-48).
7. Matt. 25:31-46 (Judgment based on person-to-person love).

B. Luke.

1. Luke 6:27-49 (Parallel to Matt. 5-7).

2. Luke 11:37-44 (Note especially verses 41 and 42).
3. Luke 12:33 (Compare with Matt. 6:20, 33; 19:21).

C. John.
1. John 14:21-23 (Notice who dwells within us when we love).
2. John 15:8-13 (Note especially verses 10-12).
3. John 15:17 (The secret of much fruit).
4. John 14-15 (Compare this passage with 1 John 4:12 and Isa. 58).

D. Acts.
1. Acts 20:36-38.

E. Romans.
1. Rom. 1:18, 19; 29-31 (Notice that hardness of heart is the end result of sin's process—compare this with the softening process seen in 1 John 4:7-21 and Col. 3:12-25).
2. Rom. 12:9, 10, 16, 21 and 14:17-19.
3. Rom. 13:8-14 (Compare with Gal. 5:1-14).
4. Rom. 14:1-15:7 (Note especially Rom. 15:7).

F. 1 Corinthians.
1. 1 Cor. 7:19 (Compare with Gal. 5:6).
2. 1 Cor. 13:1-14:1 (Pursue *love*—"Make love your aim").

G. 2 Corinthians.
1. 2 Cor. 9:1-15 (The grace of giving and sharing in love).

H. Galatians.
1. Gal. 5:14-6:3.
I. Ephesians.
1. Eph. 4:1-3 and 4:15, 16. (Note especially Eph. 4:17-19. This passage shows the process behind the hardening of the heart).
2. Eph. 5:1, 2; 5:25, 28 and 33.
J. Philippians.
1. Phil. 1:9-11.
K. Colossians.
1. Col. 1:4 (Compare with 1 John 3:23 and 1 Thess. 1:3).
2. Col. 2:2 (Compare with Phil. 2:1-15).
3. Col. 3:1-23 (Note: You set your affections on things above by demonstrating His love to the brethren).
L. 1 Thessalonians.
1. 1 Thess. 3:12, 13 (Note the definition for "holiness" from the KJV).
2. 1 Thess. 4:9, 10.
3. 1 Thess. 5:8 (See also 1 Thess. 2:19, 20).
M. 1 Timothy.
1. 1 Tim. 1:5 (Now the end of the "charge" ["commandment" - KJV] is love—Love which issues out of a pure heart, a good conscience and a true faith).
2. 1 Tim. 5:9, 10; 6:3 (Note, "wholesome words").
N. Titus.
1. Titus 1:15, 16; 2:7, 8-14—"Zealous unto good works" (3:14).

O. Hebrews.
1. Heb. 10:24 and 13:1.

P. James.
1. James 1:19-25; 2:1-13 (Compare 2:13 with Matt. 5:7).
2. James 3:10-18; 4:11.

Q. 1 Peter.
1. 1 Pet. 1:22 (Key passage—note "unto" implying "direction toward").
2. 1 Pet. 2:18-4:1 (Love for one's enemies).
3. 1 Pet. 4:8.

R. 2 Peter.
1. 2 Pet. 1:3-15.

S. 1 John.
1. 1 John 1:3, 5, 7; 4:7-5:2 (All of 1 John emphasizes the person-to-person love which results from the love of God experienced in our hearts).
2. 1 John 3:10-23.

(There are many more emphases in the New Testament which come under the "umbrella" of love's behavior such as purity of speech and conduct, etc., but enough are given here to show it as a consistent emphasis.)

OLD TESTAMENT PASSAGES

A. Deuteronomy—the whole book is worthy of study as being foundational for all the other passages. (For example, read Deut. 10:12-22).

B. Job.
1. Job 24 and 31.

2. Job 29 (Compare God's estimate of Job in 1:1 and 1:8).

C. Psalms.
1. Ps. 15 (The pure in heart).
2. Ps. 41:1-3.

D. Proverbs.
1. Prov. 1:7 and 8:13 (Key passages).
2. Prov. 3:3.
3. Prov. 3:27, 28 (Compare with Ps. 37—the righteous man; Ps. 111—the righteousness of God; and Ps. 112—the righteous deeds of the righteous man).
4. Prov. 6:17-35.
5. The entire book of Proverbs is a virtual treasure-trove of these truths. Most of the book concerns right conduct between individuals and sincere speech, etc. Such integrity is based on love.

E. Isaiah.
1. Isa. 1:10-20.
2. Isa. 5:1-25.
3. Isa. 58 (Note that God desires "mercy" more than He desires "sacrifice").
4. Isa. 59:1-15.

F. Jeremiah.
1. Jer. 7:1-34.
2. Jer. 31:31-34 (Compare with Ezek. 36:25-38).

G. Ezekiel.
1. Compare Ezek. 18:19-32 with Ezek. 33:10-32.
2. Ezek. 34.

H. Amos.
   1. Amos 4:1-3 (Compare with Ezek. 16:49, 50).
I. Micah.
   1. Mic. 6:6-8 (These are key verses which were later quoted by Jesus in Matt. 23:28).
J. Zechariah.
   1. Zech. 7:8-14.
   2. Zech. 8:16 (Compare with James 1:27).

For free information on how to receive
the international magazine

LOGOS JOURNAL

also Book Catalog

Write: Information - LOGOS JOURNAL CATALOG
Box 191
Plainfield, NJ 07061